Poetry, Narrative, History

THE BUCKNELL LECTURES IN LITERARY THEORY
General Editors: Michael Payne and Harold Schweizer

The lectures in this series explore some of the fundamental changes in literary studies that have occurred during the past thirty years in response to new work in feminism, Marxism, psychoanalysis, and deconstruction. They assess the impact of these changes and examine specific texts in the light of this new work. Each volume in the series includes a critical assessment of the lecturer's own publications, an interview, and a comprehensive bibliography.

Frank Kermode   *Poetry, Narrative, History*
Terry Eagleton   *The Significance of Theory*
Toril Moi   *Feminist Theory and Simone de Beauvoir*

Poetry,
Narrative,
History

Frank Kermode

Basil Blackwell

First published 1990

Basil Blackwell Ltd
108 Cowley Road, Oxford, OX4 1JF, UK

Basil Blackwell, Inc.
3 Cambridge Center
Cambridge, Massachusetts 02142, USA

British Library Cataloguing in Publication Data

A CIP catalogue record for this book is available from the British Library.

Library of Congress Cataloging in Publication Data
Kermode, Frank, 1919–
    Poetry, narrative, history / Frank Kermode.
        p.   cm. — (The Bucknell lectures in literary theory)
    Includes bibliographical references.
    ISBN 0–631–17264–5 — ISBN 0–631–17265–3 (pbk.)
    1. Poetry—History and criticism.   2. History and literature.
3. Narration (Rhetoric)   I. Title.   II. Series.
PN1080.K47   1989   89–38728
809.1—dc20   CIP

Typeset in 11 on 13 pt Plantin
by Photo·graphics, Honiton, Devon
Printed in Great Britain by Billing & Sons Ltd, Worcester

Contents

Preface

Fundamental and far-reaching changes in literary studies, often compared to paradigmatic shifts in the sciences, have been taking place during the last thirty years. These changes have included enlarging the literary canon not only to include novels, poems and plays by writers whose race, gender or nationality had marginalized their work, but also to include texts by philosophers, psychoanalysts, historians, anthropologists, social and religious thinkers, who previously were studied by critics merely as 'background'. The stance of the critic and student of literature is also now more in question than ever before. In 1951 it was possible for Cleanth Brooks to declare with confidence that the critic's job was to describe and evaluate literary objects, implying the relevance for criticism of the model of scientific objectivity while leaving unasked questions concerning significant issues in scientific theory, such as complementarity, indeterminacy and the use of metaphor. Now the possibility of value-free scepticism is itself in doubt as many feminist, Marxist and psychoanalytic theorists have stressed the inescapability of ideology and the consequent obligation of teachers and students of literature to declare their political, axiological and aesthetic positions in order to make those positions conscious and available for examination. Such expansion and deepening of literary studies has, for many critics, revitalized their field.

Those for whom the theoretical revolution has been regenerative would readily echo, and apply to criticism, Lacan's call to revitalize psychoanalysis: 'I consider it to be an urgent task to disengage from concepts that are being deadened by routine use the meaning that they regain both from a re-examination of their history and from a reflexion on their subjective foundations. That, no doubt, is the teacher's prime function.'

Many practising writers and teachers of literature, however, see recent developments in literary theory as dangerous and anti-humanistic. They would insist that displacement of the centrality of the word, claims for the 'death of the author' emphasis upon gaps and incapacities in language, and indiscriminate opening of the canon threaten to marginalize literature itself. In this view the advance of theory is possible only because of literature's retreat in the face of aggressive moves by Marxism, feminism, deconstruction and psychoanalysis. Furthermore, at a time of militant conservatism and the dominance of corporate values in America and Western Europe, literary theory threatens to diminish further the declining audience for literature and criticism. Theoretical books are difficult to read; they usually assume that their readers possess knowledge that few have who have received a traditional literary education; they often require massive reassessments of language, meaning and the world; they seem to draw their life from suspect branches of other disciplines: professional philosophers usually avoid Derrida; psychoanalysts dismiss Freud as unscientific; Lacan was excommunicated even by the International Psycho-Analytical Association.

The volumes in this series record part of the attempt at Bucknell University to sustain conversation about changes in literary studies, the impact of those changes on literary art and the significance of literary theory for the humanities and human sciences. A generous grant from the Andrew W. Mellon Foundation has made possible a five-year series of visiting lectureships by internationally known participants in the reshaping of literary studies. Each volume includes a comprehensive introduction to the published work of the lecturer, the two Bucknell Lectures, an interview and a comprehensive bibliography.

Introduction

In the preface to *Continuities* (1968) Frank Kermode laments that literary journalism has become a despised or neglected art. At the same time, he sustains the hope that it can be revived and its fortunes reversed. Although Kermode has himself written for a broad general audience with great success for more than thirty years, he has also had a deep impact on biblical, Renaissance and modern literary scholarship, while managing to be in the vanguard of the latest theoretical developments that have reshaped the humanities since the Second World War. Despite the fundamental theoretical differences that distinguish their work, Frank Kermode's career is closely parallel to that of Northrop Frye. They have both profoundly influenced recent criticism and scholarship on the Bible, Spenser, Shakespeare, Milton, the English Romantics and the classic moderns (especially Yeats, Eliot and Stevens). They have taken upon themselves the broad cultural responsibilities of literary criticism that Matthew Arnold and T. S. Eliot once assumed. They have made major contributions to literary theory by drawing on their extensive knowledge of sacred and secular canons, by maintaining, however modestly and ironically, a commitment to the values of liberal humanistic culture, and by promoting the intellectual and ethical freedom of the individual reader, while resisting the solipsism of bourgeois liberalism.

Beyond these superficial resemblances, however, the critical practices of Kermode and Frye diverge sharply. Their criticism on any common subject – such as their two editions of *The Tempest* or their recent books on the Bible – is fundamentally dissimilar in theory and method. What most clearly distinguishes Kermode's work is his theory of fiction. Unlike myths, he argues, fictions are self-consciously made, and their invention is an occasion for us to encounter ourselves and to reflect upon our ends. As a means 'for finding things out', for making sense of our lives, fictions 'change as the needs of sense-making change'. While myths work for stability, fictions promote change and call for 'conditional assent'; myths point back to a lost past, fictions to the here and now (*SE*, p. 39). By turning away from history and the presence of fictions in the here and now, Frye, in Kermode's judgement, fatally reduces the actual complexity of texts. Kermode, on the other hand, in his 1962 Warton Lecture, 'Spenser and the Allegorists', offers a bold and powerful argument for rejecting the view that 'Spenser sacrifices actuality, contemporaneity, to the archetypes'. Spenser 'does not convert event into myth, but myth into event. His mood is acceptance; he welcomes history, not seeking to lose his own time in some transhistorical pattern' (*SSD*, p. 22). The ahistoricism of Frye, Joseph Campbell, Austin Farrer, and 'the dark side' of D. H. Lawrence represented by *Apocalypse* have contributed not only to the promoting of myth but also to the 'dislodging' of Spenser from the secular canon 'with no fuss at all' (*SSD*, p. 12). At the same time, the substitution of mythic unconsciousness for self-critical fiction has unwittingly participated in 'the rebirth of the medieval eschatological fantasies' (*SSD*, p. 23) from which Nazism and anti-Semitism draw their terrible life. Kermode was to return to this point later in *The Sense of an Ending* (1967): 'Anti-Semitism is a fiction of escape which tells you nothing about death but projects it onto others. . . . In this sense anti-Semitism is a degenerate fiction, a myth' (*SE*, p. 39).

Although he has written careful critiques of Frye's work, especially of *Anatomy of Criticism*, *A Natural Perspective* and *The Great Code*, Kermode has not formulated his theory of fiction merely in response to a worthy antagonist but has instead developed it out of his own detailed editorial work. His first book was an edition of *English Pastoral Poetry* (1952), which is still in print and remains unrivalled, the editors of *The Penguin Book of English Pastoral Verse* having unfortunately ignored Kermode's warning that no genuine understanding of English pastoral is possible without acquaintance with classical and foreign poets. In his superb introduction to his edition, Kermode offers a potent theory of pastoral, building on what he calls the 'speculative and exciting inquiry' (*EPP*, p. 254) of William Empson's *Some Versions of Pastoral*:

The first condition of pastoral poetry is that there should be a sharp difference between two ways of life, the rustic and the urban. The city is an artificial product, and the pastoral poet invariably lives in it, or is the product of its schools and universities. Considerable animosity may exist between the townsman and the countryman. Thus the 'primitive' may be sceptical about the justice of a state of affairs which makes him live under rude conditions while the town-poet lives in polite society. On the other hand, the town- or court-poet has a certain contempt for the peasant (sometimes very strong); and both primitive and court-poet write verse which reflects these attitudes. Occasionally there is a certain similarity of subject. Townsman and rustic alike may consider the idea that at a remote period in history nature gave forth her fruits without the aid of man's labour and worship. Perhaps, somewhere, she still does so. This idea that the world has been a better place and that men have degenerated is remarkably widespread, and a regular feature of pastoral poetry. . . . The first condition of Pastoral is that it is an urban product. (*EPP*, p. 14)

This view of pastoral is not only an account of a poetic form; it contains within it a cultural vision that sees the literary form as vitalizing the myth of the Golden Age with the primary impulse of 'human resentment at the conditions and struggles of life . . . in almost every recorded culture from Mycenaean to American Negro' (*EPP*, pp. 14–15). Two years later, in his Arden edition of *The Tempest* (1954), which is one of the finest volumes in that series, Kermode further develops his theory of pastoral. In its concern with the opposition of nature and art, *The Tempest* brings together a literary tradition, which extends back through the Sixth Book of the *Faerie Queene*, with the Bermuda pamphlets of 1609 that gave 'an extraordinary actuality' to ancient poetic and philosophical problems (*T*, p. xxv). Kermode anticipates by thirty years the now current historically materialist considerations of the play by seeing the pamphlets, the play and Shakespeare's own extensive readings in New World travel literature as a 'somewhat sophistical argument for the propriety of usurping the rights of native populations' (*T*, p. xxxi). The test of viable fiction is as much how it is used and the measure of self-awareness it promotes as its internal coherence.

The mutually constituting realities of art and nature, text and world are also the central concerns of *Romantic Image* (1957). Published in the same year as Frye's *Anatomy of Criticism*, Kermode's book is concerned with the history and survival of the Romantic conception of the artist, whose vision of radiant truth isolates him from the modern industrial state and the modern middle class. Yeats is the focal point of Kermode's argument not only because of Yeats's full sense of the ecstasy and the pain of the Romantic image, but also because of Yeats's aesthetic utilitarianism, which Kermode affirms: 'Art was always made *for* men who habitually move in space and time, whose language is propelled onward by verbs, who cannot always be asked to respect the new enclosure laws of poetry, or such forbidding notices as "No road through to action" ' (*RI*, p. 161). Two subordinate topics that will become central concerns in his later books rise to the surface toward the end of Kermode's argument: the relationship of critical discourse to the image or the supreme fiction; and the ways critics and poets shape the secular canon. In a detailed critique of Eliot's 'dissociation of sensibility', Kermode reflects upon the historiography of poets and critics when 'they seek . . . a historical period possessing the qualities they postulate for the Image: unity, indissociability; qualities which, though passionately desired, are, they say, uniquely hard to come by in the modern world' (*RI*, p. 145). As often happens in Kermode's books, he argues both a positive and a negative case at once. Here the counter-argument to the thesis that the radiant image isolates the artist from the world is that the image is holistic only because it is purposefully but perversely partial, selective, cut off. Literary history is written by the poet and the critic to serve that partial image. Finally, the word must be returned to the world, for only there can a road through to action be found. *Romantic Image* ends with the prophecy both of the death of 'the Symbolist historical doctrine of dissociation of sensibility' and the recovery of Milton and especially of *Paradise Lost*, 'perhaps the richest and most intricately beautiful poem in the world' (*RI*, p. 165).

In 1960 Kermode edited *The Living Milton* as part of an effort to 'liberate' the poet from the ban imposed by a succession of Symbolist critics culminating in T. S. Eliot, who argued that Milton was in every way unlikeable, that his influence has always been for the worst, that he is fundamentally unsensual and that he is absurdly and ubiquitously revolutionary. In 'Milton II', reprinted in Kermode's edition of *Selected Prose of T. S. Eliot*, the case against Milton reaches its climax: 'We cannot, in literature, any more than in the rest of life, live in a perpetual state of revolution' (*SP*, p. 273). Kermode's own contribution to *The Living Milton* brilliantly refutes Eliot's case, not so much by attacking Eliot directly – or even A. J. A. Waldock, who substitutes for Eliot in Kermode's rebuttal – as by developing the argument that *Paradise Lost* embodies 'life in a great symbolic attitude' (*LM*, p. 86). Rather than banning Milton, Kermode argues, the modern reader is in the best position to read him. Equipped as we are with a taste for the primitive that has been cultivated from Herder, Rousseau and Wordsworth to Nietzsche, Cassirer and Pound; schooled in an open tradition of biblical interpretation; prepared to accept works of art that insist on the human capacity for pleasure; experienced in poetry's primary effect on the senses; chastened by a universal sense of irrecoverable loss; and enlightened by elaborate novelistic developments in the use of point of view, we should be prepared to consider 'Milton in a characteristically modern view of literature, to treat him as a living poet' (*LM*, p. ix). Although it is addressed primarily to the undifferentiated modern reader and modern poet, Kermode's 'Adam Unparadised' has had a profound impact on subsequent Milton studies, from Anne Davidson Ferry's *Milton's Epic Voice* (1963) and Stanley Fish's *Surprised by Sin: The Reader in Paradise Lost* (1967) to Sanford Budick's *The Dividing Muse* (1985) and Christopher Kendrick's *Milton: A Study in Ideology and Form* (1986). Like his essays on Spenser and Shakespeare, his monographs on Stevens and Lawrence, and his recent biblical studies, Kermode's Milton essay is both a lucid introduction to its subject and a rich source of ideas for later critics to develop.

Although they form a small portion of his professional writings, Kermode's comments on the sixties – Vietnam, the student movement, Paris 1968 – situate his sequence of books from *Romantic Image* to *The Sense of an Ending*. As a professor, parent and critic committed to the social use of literature, he was hit hard by those events, as were thousands of other thinkers around the world. One product of this period was his 'guru' Modern Masters Series, another was his sustained reassessment of institutional authority, which he had questioned from the beginning of his career. In his most recent book, *History and Value*, Kermode's declaration of 'the boldness to transgress, to break moulds and conventions' (*HV*, p. viii) reads like a personal manifesto.

Kermode's studies in the fifties and sixties of fiction, image and their uses led him to raise powerful theoretical questions about the survival of the classic and the pluralism of interpretation. Such questions are at the heart of his simultaneous interests in the Renaissance (which recovers and reinterprets classic and biblical texts), the modernist movement (which celebrates the artist's vision but threatens to isolate him from communities past and present) and biblical tradition (which by turns affirms vision, canon formation and institutionally sanctioned interpretation that attempts to conceal its power behind the separation of the sacred from the secular). If these theoretical issues slumbered in an uneasy latency in Kermode's earlier work, they awake to become fully manifest in his T. S. Eliot Memorial Lectures of 1975, *The Classic*. The argument of these four lectures takes shape against the background of Eliot's paper 'What Is a Classic?' (1944). Eliot observed that a classic can be known only by hindsight 'and in historical perspective', and it is the product of a mature mind and a mature civilization, and that 'the maturity of a literature is the reflection of that of the society in which it is produced' (*SP*, pp. 116–17). Eliot's historical and social emphasis is congenial to Kermode's thought, but the heavily privileged word 'maturity' opens Eliot up for a modernist critique in a manner similar to the subtle polemic of *Romantic Image*.

Kermode begins by showing that Eliot's view of the

classic is inseparable from his notion of empire that leads
to secular canon formation in terms of doctrine, style and
choices of authority. Such chosen authorities were called
classics by Aulus Gellius in the second century, who argued
that a classic writer is distinguished from the rabble and
that classics need to be of some antiquity, thus anticipating
two of Eliot's principal points. Kermode, however,
emphasizes the idea that the doctrine of the classic assumes
that the ancient can be made contemporaneous with the
modern by 'strategies of accommodation'. Indeed, the
word *modern*, apparently introduced in the sixth century,
made it possible to claim two centuries later that Charle-
magne had instituted a *saeculum modernum*, a renovation
of classical models. The classic as a meeting point of
ancient authority and modern accommodation is of major
importance in the criticism of Sainte-Beuve, who sees in
Virgil the ability to make an ancient subject relevant to
his own historical moment. Matthew Arnold disagrees with
Sainte-Beuve's view of Virgil, arguing that a classic should
enable us to think of its age and our own together. T. S.
Eliot develops his idea of the classic out of Sainte-Beuve
and Arnold, seeing the modern as a renovation of the
classic instead of something totally new. Having traced the
dialectic of classic and modern from Sainte-Beuve to Eliot,
Kermode concludes with the observation, 'The books we
call classics possess intrinsic qualities that endure, but
possess also an openness to accommodation which keeps
them alive under endlessly varying dispositions' (*C*, p. 44).
The processes of canon formation and of hermeneutics are
inextricably related, as the rest of these lectures and most
of Kermode's writing since 1975 demonstrate.

   The second lecture in this volume traces the history of
the imperial classic and the myth of Augustanism into the
poems of Marvell, who amends the imperial classic with
secular, modern wit, and of Milton, who abandons them
for the alternatives of Hebraic scripture. For Milton, Israel
is the *figura* of the British Empire and the Scriptures are

its classic. English Augustanism, however, is the exfoliation of Marvell's modernism; and in Addison the new historiography of the eighteenth century generates an ideal way with the classic: the reader is to get as close as possible to reading the classic as its contemporaries did. Although contemporary hermeneutical theory is more likely to claim its descent from Schleiermacher, Kermode makes a convincing case for the continued vitality of Addison's distinction between *hermeneutics* on the one hand, which regards the classic as a closed book waiting to be pried open by learning and thinks of meaning as contemporary with the author, and *accommodation*, on the other hand, which regards the classic as an open text generating new readings and thinks of meaning as contemporary with the reader. In his third and fourth lectures Kermode sustains these distinctions through detailed readings of Hawthorne's major novels and through a careful investigation of alternative readings of *Wuthering Heights*. He concludes by affirming the secularization and pluralization of the classic. Its essence, he argues, remains 'available to us under our dispositions, in the aspect of time' (*C*, p. 141). For the modern critic, Addison's hermeneutics and accommodation are both essential.

Having redeemed the secular classic for modernism in his Eliot Lectures, Kermode turns directly to the Bible in his Norton Lectures, *The Genesis of Secrecy* (1979). He argues that hermeneutics, the art or philosophy of interpretation, recognizes not only the distinction between manifest and latent sense but also claims the superiority of the latent. Within New Testament Christianity and the Gospel of Mark especially, this means that the insiders know or have access to the latent sense, while the outsiders know only the manifest. To forsake the manifest or the carnal for the latent or the spiritual is to become involved in hermeneutics. In this tradition the highest form of interpretation is the most intuitive, the most free of theory or doctrine. 'Carnal readings are much the same. Spiritual readings arc all different' (*GS*, p. 9). Interpretation involves, first of all, selection and emphasis, which includes also exclusion. The Gospels are a sequence of such interpretive acts: Mark interprets the earliest oral traditions concerning Jesus; Matthew and Luke interpret Mark. Tradition, then, can be seen as a 'productive encounter between a text and a reader' (*GS*, p. 40) and interpretation as 'the linking of a new discourse to the discourse of the text' (*GS*, p. 44). Midrash is an interpretive tradition (and a body of texts) that works by augmenting narrative in order to embody the interpretation of a prior text in a form other than commentary. One manifestation of midrashic interpretation is typology, the conviction that the earlier text holds in disguised form promises that are fulfilled in a later text. The New Testament, then, may be thought of as midrash on Hebrew scripture, but in an extreme sense: 'The entire Jewish Bible was to be sacrificed to the validation of the historicity of the Gospels; yet its whole authority was needed to establish that historicity' (*GS*, p. 107). Given such processes of the generation of texts from acts of interpretation, the historical truth of the narrative comes not from the text but from the institution that validates a given interpretation of the text. Kermode affirms Spinoza's observation of critical differences between the meaning and the truth of a text.'All modern interpretation . . . involves some effort to divorce meaning and truth' (*GS*, p. 122).

Kermode's argument seems impishly designed to send shock waves through literary and biblical studies simultaneously. Although a few apostates had abandoned the formalist doctrines of American New Criticism by 1979, literary study was accepted almost without question as a secular enterprise in which scepticism was the primary article of faith. Even students of medieval English literature approached religious topics warily, as the continuing controversial reception of D. W. Robertson's *A Preface to Chaucer* (1962) indicates. At the same time that he labours to bring the methods of secular criticism to sacred texts, however, Kermode juxtaposes the narrative techniques of the Gospels with those of James, Joyce, Henry Green and Pynchon. In his contributions to *The Literary Guide to the Bible* (1987), Kermode is necessarily less kaleidoscopic and more telescopic than in his Norton Lectures. But in his need to look back to ancient processes of canon formation, Kermode keeps reminding us of how the perpetually receding present keeps us running forward in order to get a sense of the past. In addition to supplying the general introduction to the New Testament and articles on Matthew and John (two of his finest essays), Kermode also writes for this volume an appendix on the canon, which includes this important passage:

> We can now specify certain characteristics of the mythical or magical view of the canon. Regardless of innumerable historical vicissitudes, redactions, interpolations, and corruptions, the canonical text is held to be externally fixed, unalterable, and of such immeasurable interpretative potential that it remains, despite its unaltered state, sufficient for all future times. This perpetual applicability is established by a continuing tradition of interpretation, as the relevance of old texts to new times always is. Interpretation is controlled by changing rules but is remarkably free, for the canonical book, itself fixed in time and probably in a dead language, has to be made relevant to an unforeseen future. It must prefigure history: hence we have typological interpretations. The book becomes a mythical model of the world: the Torah is said to be identical with the Creation, the Christian Bible becomes the twin of the Book of Nature. And the exploration of these world-books requires interpreters who can study the subtle hidden structures just as physicists and chemists (or their ancestors, the alchemists and astrologers and magicians) studied the created world. (*LGB*, pp. 605–6)

These words extend the argument of *The Classic* in their

advocacy of a synthesis of hermeneutics and accommodation, but the resonance of the argument is deeper because
of its implications for structures of knowledge that bind
literature, religion and science in a common enterprise.

Kermode's thinking progresses from book to book by
making manifest in a subsequent argument what had been
latent in a previous one. Thus, almost in spite of the bold
innovations in his thought at any given stage of his career,
Kermode's work is also dynamically cumulative. This
organic coherence is most apparent in his latest book,
History and Value (1988), which returns to the social vision
of pastoral that he articulated in 1952. This book also
revives the desire, which he discovered in Yeats, to
overcome the artist's isolation – the price of the Romantic
image – in order to find a 'road back to action', and it
further explores the complementarity of hermeneutics and
accommodation, which Kermode uncovered in classical,
biblical and modernist literature. In a more direct way
History and Value may be seen as the completion to the
argument of the Wellek Lectures, *Forms of Attention* (1985),
where Kermode asked, 'By what means do we attribute
value to works of art, and how do our valuations affect
our ways of attending to them?' (*FA*, p. xiii). In sketching
an answer to this question, he first outlines the roles of
opinion (or ignorance) in Swinburne and Pater and
knowledge in Herbert Horne and Aby Warburg that led
to the recovery of Botticelli's reputation as a great painter.
In a second lecture Kermode performs a post-modernist
interpretation on *Hamlet* in the manner of Derrida and de
Man in order to show both that a canonical text is
'omnisignificant' and that its place in the canon requires
its being subject to perpetually new hermeneutical acts. In
his final Wellek Lecture Kermode both champions the
theoretical pluralism of contemporary thought about texts,
in which knowledge and opinion play their parts, and
commits that pluralism to maintaining the vitality of the
literary canon. Implicit in this argument is his conviction

that the shape of the canon is the product of the history and value of forms of attention, which can recover lost or neglected works and maintain the sense of their 'omnisignificance'. *Forms of Attention* and *History and Value* are more daringly personal than Kermode's earlier books. In the Wellek Lectures he declares himself for contemporary theory as a means of keeping attention focused on the literature that matters. In *History and Value* he returns to the literature of his youth, to the poetry and fiction of the thirties, in order to examine how fifty years of modern history have altered the perception of the value of that literature.

History and Value combines two series of lectures in a single volume, the newly established Clarendon Lectures at Oxford and the Lord Northcliffe Lectures at University College, London. Like most of his books, this one has an oral, performative dimension; but in the case of the Clarendon Lectures (chapters 1–4) this rhetorical quality is more pronounced. Here Kermode seems self-reflectively to be lecturing to an audience of 'others'. As a man in his late sixties, he addresses an audience 'largely of people who were about twenty' (*HV*, p. vii) concerning a literature that was important to him when he was their age but which has since come to be undervalued. As most recently a London and Cambridge man, he addresses an Oxford audience; and as a man whose family 'managed well on £3' a week (*HV*, p. 47), he speaks to a largely affluent assembly. These dimensions of otherness are relevant to his argument and inform its tone and axiology. Kermode's thesis is that the proletarian literature of the thirties was a pastoral literature in the sense in which he defined pastoral in his study of 1952. Pastoral is based on the distinction between two ways of life. The writer of pastoral looks at his subject, seeing it as an other separated from the writer by an ironic gulf that the imagination attempts to cross in an effort to realize its subject while never forgetting the distance of class and value that constitutes the gulf. Kermode begins his account of this literature in a surprising way. During his wartime journey to New York in 1943 as the only passenger on a French liner, he accidently came across *Nya*, the first novel by Stephen Haggard, which deals with the love of a sexually inexperienced young yachtsman for a thirteen-year-old girl who has recently been transplanted from colonial Africa to England. *Nya*, which has just been reissued by Oxford University Press with an introduction by Kermode, unexpectedly and indirectly introduces the subject of proletarian literature in which the bourgeois writer imaginatively attempts to cross the gulf of class not only to write about his proletarian subjects but to love them as well. In the fiction of Edward Upward, Lewis Jones, and in the writings of Christopher Caudwell the subject is 'the loving surrender to necessity required by Communism – a kind of loving which assumes the economic and psychic oneness of humanity' (*HV*, p. 40). Kermode enlists his original audience (and now his readers) in a collective effort of sympathetic imagination to cross the gulf of class and time to recover the value of this literature, which contemporary politics, ideology, and bourgeois taste have made virtually inaccessible: 'To know the ordinary other one is forced to be extraordinary, which makes it difficult to join the ordinary' (*HV*, p. 50). Although he has here carefully avoided much overt reference to his recent biblical studies, Kermode's description of the efforts of bourgeois socialists to cross the gulf in order to write about and to love the proletariat builds on the argument of *The Genesis of Secrecy*. Like the Gospel of Mark, the literature of the thirties rests on the distinction between insiders and outsiders, between the circumcised and uncircumcised ear: 'In art, the core of cultured persons will if only from habit prefer the more distant, mythical, pastoral view to the factuality of the proletarian novel, as written by insiders' (*HV*, p. 93). Perhaps the final gesture of distancing proletarian factuality is the definitive renunciation of this work, whether by

Auden, who renounces some of his own poems for ideological reasons, or by current academic Marxists, who prefer a hermeneutic of suspicion to one of redemption, or by the general reader, who prefers to accept the myth of the embarrassing incompetence of these writers to the effort to redeem them.

Although it begins with an effort to recover the literature of Kermode's youth, *History and Value* engages the most recent issues of literary theory by his usual method of double polemic. In *Forms of Attention* Kermode affirms post–modernist theory but sees its most important use as preserving the traditional canon. Here, the ideology of canon formation is his subject. Kermode's approach to this subject is, however, disarmingly personal and moving, though no less theoretically sophisticated than the arguments of Terry Eagleton, Frederic Jameson and Houston Baker (the unnamed author of the passage on pp. 113–14) that it challenges. This latest work, like its distinguished predecessors, is an exercise of historical imagination at its best. It proceeds from what used to be called 'primary' literary texts to confront the most recent controversial issues in literary theory, and it achieves its end with the same lucidity and humane generosity that have distinguished Kermode's entire career.

Michael Payne

In Walter Benjamin's 'Der Erzähler'[1] (The Narrator) there is the story of Psammenit, king of the Egyptians, who was defeated and captured by the Persian king Kambyses. In order to humiliate his prisoner king, Kambyses had Psammenit stand alongside the road on which the Persians displayed their Egyptian prisoners. Thus Psammenit was forced to witness the enslavement of his daughter, who walked by with a pitcher on her head. His son was also led by to be executed. Psammenit kept his eyes on the ground and uttered not a word. Soon afterwards Psammenit recognized one of his old servants in the train of prisoners and only now did Psammenit express his grief, beating himself and wailing loudly. Benjamin tells the story to point out 'wie es mit der wahren Erzählung steht' (what a true narrative is). Montaigne is said to have asked why Psammenit showed his grief only at the sight of his servant. But Montaigne's answer, quoted by Benjamin, is only one of many, and that is the potential of Benjamin's 'true narrative'. Like Montaigne's *Essays*, which are 'varied exploration[s] of the innumerable styles of being a self',[2] all narratives contain plurality, as the story of Psammenit demonstrates, in offering a generic form to retain secrets and the inexhaustible meanings of Psammenit's grief. Literary narratives are like the kernels, as Benjamin tells us, kept in airtight chambers of the Egyptian pyramids and retaining their power of germination to this day.

Benjamin's allegory of a literary narrative as a kernel hidden in a pyramid and added as an afterthought to the story of Psammenit functions not only as an allegory of literary value but also, perhaps unintentionally, as an allegory of hermeneutic curiosity, and these two have a problematic relationship. The kernel is the symbol of a secret, embedded and preserved in a literary narrative that has been revealed. Once discovered, the 'airtight chamber' where it has lain for 'thousands of years' is broken open, the kernel must yield its secret, the time of its concealment has come to an end. Nor are there any of the multiple meanings that Benjamin claimed inherent in the story of Psammenit. The kernel will presumably grow into a plant. As an allegory of hermeneutic curiosity the story of the kernel reveals that somewhere below the multiple meanings of Psammenit's grief is a desire for closure. Both Benjamin's story of Psammenit and the allegory of the kernel grant the reader the fulfilment of this need. But Herodot, who wrote the story of Psammenit, 'explains nothing'. It is *our* closure that we force upon the narrative and by our closure we mean our temporality, our need for order and completion. In his illuminating interpretation of narrative, *The Genesis of Secrecy*, Frank Kermode arrives at such a moment in his reading of the Gospel of Mark: 'we cannot avoid the reflection that we ourselves are intercalated into the story . . . between the long past (which we recapitulate) and the imminent ending, which is our own, and, like Mark's, no parousia but a matter of fear and silence' (*GS*, p. 127). As we, in silence, attend the moment of the archaeologist's discovery, as when Montaigne says that Psammenit's grief found expression because it had steadily increased to overflow at the sight of the servant, the narrative partakes of two coextensive times: eternity – 'thousands of years', 'the long past' – and the time of the discovery. However, we can only see the long past from the temporal and finite perspective of the discovery. And yet, the long past, Psammenit's grief like the kernel's age are preserved as mysteries while at the same time the mysteries are discovered and revealed. Like Job, who 'sees' in the last chapter of the book what he does not understand, and like Benjamin's allegory, Kermode's interpretations participate in this paradoxical situation: as interpretations seeking to explain the secret of Psammenit's grief, which is the plurality of its meanings, the interpretation loses its expressive potential at the moment of the archaeologist's discovery, at the moment when it makes its point. What it can explain is thousands of years cancelled by discovery, the equivalent to the single meaning, to which we attend both with a sense of fulfilment but also with a sense of disappointment. Although interpretations are anachronistic and although they bar our access to the mystery of the story and to the 'thousands of years' to the kernel, 'without interpretation there would be no mystery' (*GS*, p. 126). And, similarly because of the kernel's discovery and our temporalizing forms of attention, the canon, like the pyramid, is 'still' a 'preservative' and 'still potent' (*GS*, p. 89).

'If one wanted to get a complete view of his work . . .
one would need to consider later essays as well', Frank
Kermode writes in a 1961 review of Edmund Wilson's
Axel's Castle (*PE*, p. 56). Two such 'later essays' – they
initiated the Bucknell Lectures in Literary Theory
in 1987 and are printed here for the first time – make
similar claims for Kermode. The essays are meant to add
and thereby to make more complete, as well as more
complex, a view of an unusually rich literary life. It has
been noted, not the least because Kermode's 'later essays'
keep adding to his work, that the range of his interests
and concerns over the last three decades make him one of
the most difficult literary critics to 'sum up'. One of the
reasons for this difficulty is programmatically announced
in the epigraph from Shakespeare to *Puzzles and Epiphanies*
(1962): 'Why, with the time, do I not glance aside / to
new-found methods and to compounds / strange?' In the
face of British academic conservatism, his receptivity to
German and later to French influences, from Vaihinger to
Derrida, has been exceptional and exemplary, and it
suggests that his comment on Wilson's anticipation of 'a
whole era of literary discussion' can be read as a commentary
on Kermode as well. Even as early as in his influential
essay on Milton, 'Adam Unparadised', Kermode discovers
what J. Hills Miller would call a linguistic moment: 'The
necessary deformation of language . . . shows, though with
delight, the difficulties under which we labour to repair
the ruins of our first parents' (*SSD*, p. 270). In both an
aesthetic and a thematic sense Kermode's delight makes
him into an author with style, as Roland Barthes would
say; by this we mean not primarily the fluidity and urbanity
of Kermode's style but his problematic relationship with
language and with history. His historical perspective owes
something to Gadamer's hermeneutics of tradition and the
separateness of the individual, which in turn inform

Kermode's Barthian concept of language, first as 'a kind of natural ambience wholly pervading the writer's expression', and second as 'an abstract circle of truths, outside of which alone the solid residue of an individual *logos* begins to settle'.[3] Thematically, or in ways we shall try to qualify with Barthes, Kermode's career could be seen as an epistemological quest not to solve but to circumscribe this dialectic in various hermeneutic and historical approaches. The 'crude' stylistic form of Kermode's argument in the way Barthes would use the term is 'a self sufficient language . . . which has its roots in the depths of the author's personal secret mythology'; it is not, as Barthes goes on, his historical frame of reference but the 'vertical and lonely dimension of thought'.[4] As such it is feasible to think of Kermode's work, like that of Northrop Frye's, as a literary, centripetal necessity, an inward-turning quest for a supreme fiction that is both latent and confessed (in Stevensian tones) in *The Sense of an Ending*, where Kermode points out that 'it is ourselves we encounter whenever we invent fictions' (*SE*, pp. 38–9). David Lodge succinctly points out in *The Modes of Modern Writing* that for Kermode, 'literature is not the only kind of fiction: history, theology, and even physics are also fictions';[5] but while as fictions they form part of the abstract circle of truths, their generic intersections might be read as allegories of a larger concern of narratives: their intersections with the self or with the real, or, as Barthes might say, their potential as 'a boundary and a perspective'. For Barthes's writer this is 'a frontier to overstep which alone might lead to the linguistically supernatural'.[6]

From the vantage point of such a theory of fictional peripeteia, where, however tangentially, the real intersects with the sense we make about it, Kermode constructs a fictionalist position, whose epistemology is impossible to verify because it can only be tested against other fictional genres. In *The Sense of an Ending*, with its vast ranges from the fictions of the medieval monk Adso to those of

Christopher Burney, literary history functions – like in Kermode's work as a whole – as a large system of 'the word against the word' (*SE*, p. 166), or of difference and deferral, wherein form, facts and values lack an epistemological ground. This is the central difference between Kermode's work and Frye's, which posits as its epistemological ground a pre-generic order of words. The logic by which Kermode sets the word against the word and literary works against each other is therefore always elliptical, a fiction itself with gaps and mysteries, calling only for conditional assent. Kermode's own conditional assent to the idea of the canon is evident in his most recent book, *History and Value*, where the vagueness of the word 'somehow', twice repeated, is part of the underlying argument, suggesting the unwarranted epistemology of the value we give to 'monuments'; for we must 'find ways of showing that their value *somehow* persists in our changed world'. And if 'we cannot avoid seeing them as interrelated, as of the same family by reason of their distinctive features and qualities . . . we have *somehow* to place them in relation to one another' (*HV*, p. 117, my emphasis). In his response to an article in the *Chronicle of Higher Education* which predicts Afro-American and feminist criticism as the future of literary studies, Kermode points out this critic's untheorized 'tacit admission that there is such a thing as literature and that there ought to be such a thing as a canon'. 'What we have here, is not a plan to abolish the canon but to capture it' (*HV*, p. 114). Here as elsewhere, Kermode's insistence to protect the canon from those who covet it is not simply reactionary but rather a theory of canon formation itself, a theory that is able to deconstruct the assumptions of those who have power as well as of those who do not. Hence, it is no surprise that Kermode's attention turns, in the subsequent paragraph, to the 'authority [that] has invented many myths for the protection of the canon' (*HV*, p. 115).

For what is the privileged centre from which we derive

the formative authority of sense, or of a canon, if its enabling antithesis is a Nietzschean pan of putrid soup? Kermode's epistemological compromises 'in a system where all is fiction except reality'[7] are evident in *The Sense of an Ending*, where he speaks of 'what we normally call real' (*SE*, p. 57) or of 'reality as we, from time to time, imagine it' (*SE*, p. 63). Referential assumptions like these are unacknowledged miniature fictions. While the reference establishes a mimetic system that can find something out for us, something real' (*SE*, p. 18), the mimesis collapses being itself fictive: reality, Kemode will admit later on in *The Sense of an Ending*, is only an 'apparent antithesis' to fiction, 'a human imaging of the inhuman' (*SE*, p. 105). But if here Kermode's argument turns on its own tautological parameter – everything is human except the inhuman – his epistemological weakness is the fictionalist's strength even when Kermode is not self-conscious enough to account for unreflected entanglements between his own discourse and 'our sense of reality' (*SE*, p. 57). In *The Art of Telling* he censors his own inconsistencies in E. C. Bentley for 'false complicity in his use of the phrase "the world we know" ' (*AT*, p. 57). Moreover, his pervasive use of the pronouns 'us' and 'we' suggests a homogeneity of the present that is as unfounded as would be the assertion of a determinable meaning of the past. But if this proves something about the inevitable mimetic quality of all fictions including Kermode's, or to put it differently, if it demonstrates the lack of fictional consciousness, this is the narrative's enabling, if illusory, quality – and this, in turn, proves Kermode's point about the invaluable necessity of fictional discourse or of 'the documents we value' (*HV*, p. 117). For their 'hermeneutic potential', as Paul Ricoeur has argued in a commentary on Kermode, performs these references with more subtlety: 'Is there not a hidden complicity between the "secrecy" engendered by the narrative itself – or at least by narratives like those of Mark and Kafka – and the as yet untold stories of our lives that constitute the prehistory, the background, the living imbrication from which the told story emerges?'[8] It is thus the inhuman, our subtextual prehistory, or in sum, our ignorance that allegorizes the literary text *per se*: imaginings of any referential import have unsolved secrets or gaps to which the critical intelligence attends, as Kermode puts it, with disappointment. But these difficulties are acknowledged. The argumentative progression of *The Sense of an Ending*, from early Christian apocalypse to Burney's inventions of a world from inside a prison, testifies not only to our need for form and consolation but equally to our scepticism which claims that forms are 'merely the architecture of our own cells' (although this is inexplicably questioned) (*SE*, p. 165) and consolations are always 'for the moment' (*SE*, p. 166). Kermode's own texts are relative to the literary works they discuss in the same way as fiction is to reality. Both criticism and fiction perform the function of corrigible schema. Thus, however internally consistent and historically coherent Kermode's setting up word against word and works against works, his fictionalist position is itself a theory of crisis or a fiction of criticism, because he cannot give a privileged epistemology to his own discourse. In recent books he admits that 'if the mind is an instrument for arranging the world in accordance with its own needs and desires, its arrangements must be fictive' (*FA*, p. 86). This deconstructive admission has larger ramifications beyond the immediate context of the interpreter's scepticism: '[T]he writer's "thing"', as Barthes would put it, 'his glory and his prison' in an institutional context of a conservative academy ruled by an aesthetics of linguistic transparency turns Kermode's epistemological failure into a moderate version of the romantic image, a 'private delight' whose road through to action is his 'pleasure of conformity' (*AT*, p. 130), 'a measure of [interpretive] liberty' held against 'the tacit authority of the institution' (*AT*, p. 184). Here

Kermode presents his solitary confinement with the key in his hand.

If his avowed purpose is to reverse the traditional priority of 'what is written about' and 'what is written', Kermode lends himself to this task with the admission of its difficulty (*GS*, p. 119). The productive reading which he advocates as a mediating delight between institution and privacy, or between modern and classical texts, has a historical and a philosophic dimension. Historically Kermode's heretical confrontation of the canonical Gospel of Mark with Henry Green's *Party Going*, 'not yet part of the secular canon' (*GS*, p. 5), reflects, ironically, the rabbinical doctrine which he quotes in *History and Value*: 'I join passages from the Torah with passages from the Hagiographa, and the words of the Torah glow as the day they were given at Sinai' (*HV*, p. 116). The glow produced by Kermode's textual confrontations is, of course, not the original meaning once 'given' to the Gospel of Mark but the text itself – and that leads us to the philosophical dimension of productive reading. Rather than attempting to penetrate the text to arrive at a meaning or typology, Kermode refuses transcendence, giving permission to be held up by the textual surface. The textual surface has traditionally been overlooked because only looked through, while Kermode's insistence on textual opacity or indeterminacy of meaning is, more literally and less transcendentally, a matter of inexhaustible texture. Access to meaning is thus in itself a problematic postulate, one that solicits warnings in *The Sense of an Ending* against the exclusive, single meaning of the unreflected myth which is an escape from the temporality of meaning and may justify the killing of six million Jews. On the opposite pole from myth is the interpreter's 'disappointment', his existential encounter with the text which implies impossibility of direct or authentic encounter with the world. But like Nietzsche's proposition of art as consolation, Kermode's disappointment seems wholly equivocal, implying that 'we see all delight through the eyes of Satan' (*SSD*, p. 281).

Like Satan who scorned the gate of Eden and leaped across the wall, the postulate of a problematic access to meaning allows us to enter the text anywhere (*AT*, p. 66). In *The Art of Telling* Kermode describes the gentile, unwalled character of our narratives as the French theorists' desire for 'a novel without transcendental reference' and for 'a world without God'. The text thus becomes the only existential platform on which 'it is possible to live, because it is possible to read without accepting official versions of reality' (*AT*, p. 70). If, nevertheless, in *The Sense of an Ending*, 'men die because they cannot join the beginning and the end' (*SE*, p. 64), we realize that our narratives humanize only the succession of time already begun. Because of the unavailability of what Ricoeur calls our 'untold stories', our told stories are always gentile, as Edward Said would say; they always begin in *medias res*, we enter them anywhere, they have their beginning and end outside of our interpretations. The post-lapsarian world of texts-in-time that Kermode sketches in these passages is one which, lacking authoritative structure, must be structured continually through interpretation. While myths present the world of texts as revealed like the unconcealed mysteries in Milton's paradise (*Paradise Lost*, book IV, 312), *The Genesis of Secrecy* urges us to recollect the pages scattered on the ground: 'The desires of interpreters are good because without them the world and the text are tacitly declared to be impossible; perhaps they are, but we must live as if the case were otherwise' (*GS*, p. 126). Prefaced to his fictionalist stance is, as we have noted above, the admission that 'we have to remember how difficult it is to behave as if it were correct' (*GS*, p. 118). This recalls Kermode's Nietzschean conviction that, lacking other consolations, we must live by fictions alone – but also that finally we cannot join the beginning with the end: death is inhuman and coarse (*SE*, p. 160). Fiction, to appropriate a phrase from *Forms of Attention*, 'is a manner of thinking about the world that is congenial to the thinker, and likely to sustain his project when reality is not' (*FA*, p. 87). The *inexhaustible* plurality of textuality, the *survival* of the canon and the *perpetual* modernity of ancient texts is, one speculates, 'biological or biographical, not historical' as Barthes names the properties of style, to endlessly defer that which presents no target to the mind's eye (*SE*, p. 161).

If literature exists, like the kernel in the Pyramid, in a timeless *aevum* 'participating in both the temporal and the eternal' (to borrow a term reserved for angels and novels in *The Sense of an Ending* (p. 72), the reader intersects these works on his temporal axis. Like 'a stick in a river' he is their 'moment of occurrence' but this moment, like the archaeologist's discovery, blinds him to what is eternal. He sees only, as does Kermode at the end of *Forms of Attention*, that he must 'resist the illusion that what I am saying can have any permanent rightness or value' (*FA*, p. 93); the statement is akin to the archaeologist's realization that through the discovery of the kernel he cannot claim admission to a pyramidal *aevum*. But this only confirms that criticism is an hermeneutics of impasses, of gaps and ellipses, in so far as criticism is always imaginary and temporal in its forms of attention to something that exceeds this form. In the book of that title, Kermode presents an analogue of this relationship in the aspirations of opinion to truth and of truth as a 'text-world' almost analogous to reality as we, from time to time, imagine it: 'Those endless chains of crossings of significance, those condensations and displacements to which the normative interpretation attends' (*FA*, p. 76). If disappointment is part of our forms of attention because it implies temporality, limitation, opinion, like that which Montaigne gave to the story of Psammenit, it is, if consciously entertained, the expression of an ethics of reading. We can read disappointment itself in its most literal meaning as a missed appointment with the literary *aevum* and as a confirmation of our temporality.

But in the reader's disappointment, as the German cultural philosopher Georg Simmel would say, the reader avoids the cultural tragedy. The interpretive attention returns the stabilized, materialized word of books to their restless resucitation in, and one would add, of the reader. This is the merit of Frank Kermode's work. While it is throughout an account and resolution of what Simmel would call the 'Formgegensatz . . . zwischen dem subjektiven Leben, das rastlos, aber zeitlich endlich ist, und seinen Inhalten, die, einmal geschaffen, unbeweglich, aber zeitlos gültig sind' ('the formal opposition between the subjective life, which is restless but temporal, and its contents, which, once created, are immutable but eternal').[9] Kermode's work offers a sustained theory and application of Simmel's cultural philosophy. His simultaneous confirmation of literature's age and potential for germination and his confirmation of the significance of discovery, make him into an affirmer of canonical tradition and at the same time its deconstructor. By his range of application for his theory, Kermode has not only revitalized the life of cultural values but has also shown the necessity of deconstructive attitudes towards the institutional attempts to turn cultural values into ideological possessions. Frank Lentricchia's foreword to *Forms of Attention* (1985) suggests that these concerns have remained unchanged as 'Kermode performs (on the theoretical highwire) the amazing feat of, on the one hand, going all the way with deconstruction and, on the other hand, keeping everything in its place, the canon preserved and protected.' But rather than to present his career as an amazing feat in its maintaining a paradoxical stance, one might want to insist on the necessity of an interaction between the canon and its deconstruction by claiming that Kermode preserves the canon only by going all the way with deconstruction. The two essays presented in this volume thus exemplify not a paradox but a dialectic, entertained in Frank Kermode's continuous conversations with a world of texts spanning from the Bible through Botticelli's paintings to the *nouveau roman* and recently back to the literature of his youth.

Harold Schweizer

REFERENCES

The following works by Frank Kermode are cited in the Introduction:

(Ed.), *English Pastoral Poetry: From the Beginnings to Marvell* (1952) (*EPP*).
(Ed.), *The Tempest* (1954) (*T*).
Romantic Image (1957)(RI)
(Ed.), *The Living Milton: Essays by Various Hands* (1960) (*LM*).
Puzzles and Epiphanies: Essays and Reviews 1955–1961 (1962) (*PE*).
The Sense of an Ending (1967) (*SE*).
Shakespeare, Spenser, Donne: Renaissance Essays (1971) (*SSD*).
(Ed.), *Selected Prose of T. S. Eliot* (1975) (*SP*).
The Classic (1975) (*C*).
The Genesis of Secrecy (1979) (*GS*).
The Art of Telling: Essays on Fiction (1983) (*AT*).
(Ed.), *The Literary Guide to the Bible* (1987) (*LGB*)
History and Value (1988) (*HV*).

NOTES

1 Walter Benjamin, *Illuminationen* (Frankfurt am Main: Suhrkamp, 1977).
2 Susan Sontag, *Against Interpretation and Other Essays* (New York: Octagon Books, 1982) p. 139.
3 Roland Barthes, *Writing Degree Zero*, trans. Lavers and Smith (New York: Hill and Wang) p. 9.
4 Ibid., pp. 10–11.
5 David Lodge, *The Modes of Modern Writing* (Ithaca, NY: Cornell University Press, 1977) p. 56.

6 Barthes, *Writing Degree Zero*, p. 9.
7 Frank Lentricchia, *After the New Criticism* (Chicago: University of Chicago Press, 1980) p. 36.
8 Paul Ricoeur, *Time and Narrative I*, trans. McLaughlin and Pellauer (Chicago: University of Chicago Press, 1984) pp. 75–6.
9 Georg Simmel, *Philosophische Kultur* (1923; repr. Berlin: Verlag Klaus Wagenbach, 1986) p. 195.

New Ways with Bible Stories

Any historical account of the rise of modern literary studies in the Bible should probably begin with Erich Auerbach's *Mimesis*, now over forty years old. But the unquestioned brilliance and originality of that work, and of the essay 'Figura' which supplements it, do not quite explain the forms taken by more recent studies of biblical narrative. They have not been directly indebted to Auerbach; the methods used, which are various, hardly resemble his, although it would probably be true to say that his bold formulation of a realism, drastically modified, that embraces the biblical narratives and the modern novel, left less conscious traces. He offered a new explanation of the importance for later literature of the Passion narratives; and what he wrote in his first chaper about the differences between the narrative style of Homer and that of the Jewish Bible must also have left a deep impression. Yet most recent studies of biblical narrative seem to come at the subject from rather different angles.

One may here offer some oversimple explanations of the motivation of this kind of scholarship. First, there is a development that is primarily Jewish. Roughly speaking, it ceased to seem necessary for Jewish critics to make an arbitrary separation between the interests and assumptions of the secular academy, and the ancient tradition of Bible study in which many of them had been trained – sometimes just on the other side of the street, though conventionally a world away from the classrooms where they studied a more modern and less sacred literature. As we shall see, the new secular interest in 'the poetics of prose' or narratology now seemed applicable to the Bible texts. And, conversely, the peculiar imaginative boldness of rabbinic commentary, the tradition, I may call it for short, of midrash, might – for some, though not for the most devout – appear to have a relationship with other forms of interpretation, at a time when philosophies and methods of interpretation had begun to grow more interesting.

There were comparable changes in attitudes towards the Christian Bible. The Gospel narratives were restored to attention *as* narratives. In his important book *The Eclipse of Biblical Narrative* published in 1974, Hans Frei showed how in the eighteenth century interest in the factuality of the narratives came to supplant consideration of them as stories; facts, not writing, were the object of scholarly consideration, and the difficult relation between history and the history-like – or, to express the point in a formula of Jean Starobinski's, between what is written and what it is written about – was forgotten. Even before Frei's book *story* was beginning to attract interest, as if, by conscious effort, one could restore the lack of differentiation between fact and story that had prevailed before 'scientific' scholarship began to treat narrative as a mere veil over historical occurrence.

This change could probably not have occurred without a prior development, the new interest in the way narratives work, one might say, in the mystery of narrative. People began to ask such questions as the following: in what sense do stories have structure? Since its primary function seems to be explanatory and persuasive, how does narrative also generate secrecy – call for so much explanation from the reader to whom it ostensibly offers explanations? Such questions may be asked of all narrative, but seem particularly appropriate to texts that have suffered many centuries of explanation. (One consequence of the wish to ask such questions was the renewal of attention to parable, and to the sort of rabbinical commentary which assumes inexhaustible stocks of secrets requiring interpretation.)

We easily assume that narrative had a natural drive towards plainness and clarity. We fall into it naturally when recounting the events of a day at the office, or a quarrel, or an encounter of any kind; it is the obvious way of explaining not only what occurred but the significance of what occurred. Of course we may also use it for concealment, or to forestall unfavourable interpretation. It was an ancient complaint against the Gnostics that by altering the narrative sequence of the Gospels they distorted the *logia*; and the idea that the Scriptures plainly offered all the explanations necessary to salvation and conduct continued to seem intuitively right. Yet such notions coexisted with the contrary assumption, common to Jew and Christian in their different ways, that there were *secrets* in the text, and that they could be brought to light only be devoted research. In this respect the rabbis and the fathers anticipated ambitious modern secular commentary, which really became possible only when certain texts were granted a pseudo-canonical status. And one might almost say that it was a rediscovery of the apparently infinite possibilities of interpretation, and a new understanding of the necessary obsolescence of commentary, partly dependent on the grant of a quasi-sacred status to secular texts, that impelled the secular scholars to look again at the originally sacred ones. And for their part, the traditional guardians of those sacred texts, their confidence in simple historical foundations impaired by two centuries of scientific scholarship, were ready to consider the new approaches to narrative that were coming from the secular critics. Bible scholars and secular critics were now able to greet one another on common ground.

On the whole they have not concerned themselves with deconstructive analysis; they use more traditional methods, though with a new intensity. But they are a varied company, and generalization is difficult. For example, it is true of some but by no means of the majority that they have simply bracketed the question of historical reference; some, perhaps most of them, regard it as inescapable. But by and large they agree that whatever else the Bible may be, it is certainly, in the first place, a form of literature; and they go on from there in their different ways. Some are indebted to the Formalist revival of the sixties, French and Soviet, some to various kinds of 'reader-response' theory, some to the severe style of narratological analysis developed in Israel. Some are eclectic. On one other matter they tend to agree. Though not disrespectful of traditional scholarship, they choose to treat narratives in the forms in which they have come down to us, ignoring speculative earlier versions (truer, perhaps, to fact) which may lie behind them.

For example, when James S. Ackerman analyses the story of Joseph's brothers in Egypt he must, if he is to discuss the text as the Bible actually offers it, account for a good deal of repetition in speech and action. In traditional scholarship this is regarded as the result of a redactor's clumsiness in conflating his sources. Ackerman does not offer to refute that view; his concern is with the *effect* of this doubling on our reading of the story. It may give emphasis, it may retard the progress of the plot in rhetorically important ways, for instance by delaying the recognition scene between Joseph and his brothers. This is so whether the doubling is the result of mere clumsiness, or whether it was done by a redactor of much greater skill than scientific criticism supposed – a writer so far from clumsy that he carefully organized the narrative to this end. Ackerman would probably agree with Robert Alter that it is usually more sensible to assume skill than inspired incompetence; but that choice makes no difference to the effect of the passage.[1]

In this respect there is not much difference between

attitudes to Old and New Testaments. For instance, it is sometimes argued that the scene in which Mary confronts Jesus before the raising of Lazarus must be an interpolation because it (partly) doubles the meeting of Jesus with Martha. This view seems to me unlikely, indeed incredible; but in any case it would not bother our modern analysts, who would simply consider the literary effect of the repetition, and probably conclude that it enhanced the value of the narrative. I shall return to that example later.

Obviously critics who look at the Bible stories in this light have had to rid themselves of an unconscious equation between antiquity and simplicity; they believe such narrative may be extremely complex in its structure and effects, yet in ways very different from modern narrative. That is why most of them refuse to ignore history; they must situate the ancient texts in the past and be mindful of the difficulties entailed by the fact that they themselves, the interpreters, exist in a historical context which is in obvious respects remote from that of the texts they are studying, though not completely cut off from it. Tzvetan Todorov has remarked that the tacit application to ancient texts of recent criteria of value – such as stylistic unity, non-contradiction, non-digression, non-repetition – can only result in a deceptive or patronizing reading; and Robert Alter adds that if we applied these criteria to such books as *Ulysses*, *The Sound and the Fury*, *Tristram Shandy* or *La Jalousie*, we should adjudge them also to be 'shoddily "redacted" literary scraps'.[2] I might add a favourite example of my own: Theodore Dreiser condemned Ford's *The Good Soldier* on the ground that Ford had found a good story but ruined it by clumsy execution – he should have begun at the beginning and gone straight on to the end.[3] Presumably we should all agree that what is inept here is the comment, not the novel. And when talking about ancient narrative it is clearly right not to be blinkered by any modern prejudice, however natural it seems. Good narratives take a great many forms at different times, and even at one time. It is in this sense that the analyst, with his attention on the text before him, is nevertheless an historian.

What I propose to do now is to give some simple instances of the modern interpretation of narratives from both the Jewish and the Christian Bibles, and then ask briefly what we are to conclude from them. I shall have to leave aside the matter of parable, though it is obviously interesting as providing the sort of narrative which is formally incomplete *without* interpretation; perhaps it is so only more obviously than other narrative, but the point, which is on some approaches central to the whole question, I have at present no time to expound. Instead I shall ask you to think first about the familiar story of David, Bathsheba and Uriah.

I choose this episode because it was the subject of a famous article by Menakhem Perry and Meir Sternberg, first published in Hebrew in 1968. In a revised form it forms the core of Sternberg's book *The Poetics of Biblical Narrative* (Bloomington, 1985). In the intervening years it attracted much comment and is the ancestor of many roughly similar studies.

The theme of the narrative, which runs from 2 Samuel 11 : 1 to 12 : 31, is murder and adultery, though until the last part of the sequence there is no open condemnation of David as adulterer and murderer. And although the story contains a variety of incidents – a military campaign, a seduction, the death of Bathsheba's husband Uriah and of her child by David and so on – it is tersely, even reticently told, even at points which seem to us to cry out for expansion and explanation. Sternberg believes that reticence is an essential aspect of the technique of such narratives; they contain significant 'gaps'. Of course all stories have gaps, total explanation would be intolerable; and it is not a new discovery that they can be subtly used. For example, Henry James and E. M. Forster both discuss the exploitation in novels of what is not expressly stated,

and after their day Robbe-Grillet developed a whole theory
and practice of the gap (and indeed of repetition and
internal contradiction). Sternberg distinguishes between
gaps and blanks, the latter being, roughly, the kind of
thing we are not told about even in Leopold Bloom's day,
simply because to tell absolutely everything would be
pathologically tedious. Gaps are different because they
have a positive part in the plot. I think myself that
Sternberg is a little too confident that he can invariably
tell a blank from a gap, but that there is a difference is
undoubted.

In this story of David and Bathsheba Sternberg finds
many rich gaps. The biblical text is omniscient – the
narrator knows what is going on in people's heads, and
even what God thinks about it all – but omniscience does
not entail omnicommunicativeness. The omniscient author
leaves gaps in which the reader must work for his own
meanings. He must work equally on repetitions and what
may look like redundant explanations, which also contribute
to the effect of the whole. I should add one more point:
Sternberg is far from being a libertarian. He believes there
are strong constraints on interpretation, and that there is
a standard of competence by which interpreters must be
measured. Like others before him, he labours to define
this 'competence'.

The rabbis knew gaps when they saw them. For example,
there is a dissonance, or a gap, between David, king of
Israel and author of the Psalms, and David, the scheming
opportunist, the lecher and the murderer of the Bathsheba
story. To fill this gap they rather uneasily suggested that
it was the custom for Israelite soldiers to divorce their
wives before going into battle so that the women, if
widowed, could escape levirate marriage; if not, they could
remarry their husbands after the war. If it can be assumed
that Uriah had done this, David can at least be acquitted
of adultery. This may not strike us as competent interpretation; the excuse does rather little for David, and it jars

with the whole context. But you see the point: something is required from the reader. Sternberg's modern gap-filling is not moral but technical. The gaps arise from the habitual reticence of the narrator, and impose on us the need to ask and answer questions: for example, does Uriah know, or suspect, that his wife has been unfaithful? Does he deduce from David's bringing him back from the front, making much of him and urging him to go home to his own house, that the king badly wants him to sleep with Bathsheba, so that the paternity of the child conceived in his absence can plausibly be attributed to Uriah? If, as seems likely, Bathsheba's bath was a post-menstrual purification, the child could not be thought to be her husband's unless he slept with her on this occasion. Or perhaps the bath is mentioned not solely to explain the arousal of David's desire at seeing Bathsheba naked, but also to indicate that he was at least not guilty of ritual impurity? This seems unlikely, but such are the questions raised by gaps. And there is an inexplicitness about the entire tale; for example, we are told very little about the early stages of the love-affair, and very little about Uriah.

There is another difficulty. What is David doing in Jerusalem watching Bathsheba when he should be with his troops? The compaign is said to be occurring 'at the time when kings go forth to battle', and David is king precisely because he is supposed to be good at leading from the front. Moreover, we are soon to learn that although he avoided the fighting he did not deny himself the glory or the plunder of conquest; for Joab, having subdued the enemy city, stood back and waited for David to occupy it formally. Are we to infer that he cheated his subordinate of the spoils, as he had cheated Uriah first of his wife and then of his life? These are possible inferences; yet little is done actively to solicit our disapproval of the king; and when God decrees the death of his child by Bathsheba we are made to feel sorry for David in his wretchedness, and surprised – even impressed? – by his extraordinary recovery when the infant actually dies.

These are samples of the Sternbergian gaps, where competent readers must go to work, each making sense of them in his or her own way. Normally we do so without reflecting on our procedures; Sternberg is trying to formalize our unexamined operations, performed because we need to do something about what we are expected to know without being told. Why did David send for Uriah? To ask forgiveness? To offer a bribe? To get him to bed with his wife? Why did Uriah stay away from her? For the reason he himself gave, namely that he should not enjoy home comforts while his comrades were still in the tented field? Or because he saw through David's trickery, and wanted him to be stuck with the paternity of the child?

It is not part of the argument that one can always fill the gaps positively. When David and Uriah are together you can ask yourself what David thinks Uriah is thinking: did he know or think that Uriah knew about him and Bathsheba? Did he think or know Uriah did not know? Was he undecided between these possibilities? And so on. We may have to content ourselves with coexistent possibilities. Sternberg's examination of these matters is always exhilarating, and it seems obvious that once you get hold of the idea that this sort of narrative works as much by what it does not as by what it does say, you are on the way to a richer understanding of biblical narrative.

One of the critics who was impressed by the Perry–Sternberg article was Robert Alter. He tells us he had long pondered another strange moment in 2 Samuel, chapter 3. Abner is sent away by David 'in peace' (*vayeleikh beshalom*), and this expression is thrice repeated; when Joab arrives he is angry about Abner's safe departure, and asks the king 'Why did you send him away, going off? ('and he is quite gone', King James Version). Here the Hebrew is *vayeleikh halokh*, a partial repetition of the formula of dismissal; and yet this time it recalls a euphemism for dying. Reading the Perry–Sternberg article, Alter came to understand that such near-repetitions make openings into the minds of the characters and the subtle movements of plot. Joab at once follows up his modification of the dismissal formula by assassinating Abner.[4]

Working on his own, Alter added much of value to this kind of narrative analysis. He reminds us how *dialogue* is used to highlight parts of the David story, with the effect that although so much else is going on, the murder of Uriah is made its central theme. Between David and Bathsheba there is a total absence of dialogue; thus adultery is relegated to the position of a contributory cause.[5] Another commentator, Adele Berlin, adds some remarks on the passivity of Bathsheba – she merely interests David by taking a conspicuous bath. We do not know whether she welcomed the king's advances or simply submitted to the royal will. She finds herself in what most women would think a difficult situation – she is an adultress, pregnant by her lover; then a widow; then a bereaved mother. But nothing is made of all this; she is not shown as feeling guilt or even grief, though David suffers both. In short, as Berlin puts it, she is a 'complete non-person, simply part of the plot'. And she doesn't acquire character until, as the wife of David and the mother of Solomon, she is involved in a succession crisis and replaced by Abishag in the old king's bed. Only then is she allowed to take part in the dialogue; no longer simply an agent, she is at last something like a person.[6]

So insights accumulate. Joel Rosenberg considers David's reply to Nathan's parable: the rich man, he says, should be made to pay the value of the poor man's ewe four times over (12: 1ff.). This is not merely involuntary self-condemnation but unconscious prophecy; for David will pay four times over for the theft of Uriah's wife. Amnon will rape Tamar and be murdered by Absalom; Absalom will be killed by Joab, who had earlier dispatched Uriah;

and Adonijah will die as a direct consequence of Bathsheba's intercession with her son Solomon on his behalf.[7]

These modern commentators do not presume that they are the first to notice the characteristics they discuss; they are only trying to give more formal accounts of them. One could accumulate evidence to show that earlier commentators had dealt with the reticences of the story – and with the moral difficulties they create – in ways that seemed equally suitable to *them*. The Christian tradition used allegory as a solvent or gap-filler: Bathsheba's bath was an allegory of baptism; David's polygamy a figure for the union of many diverse peoples in the faith. But allegory of this kind can solve anything; and for some early commentators the questions to be answered were more human and more commonplace. What was Bathsheba doing on the roof? Was she being immodest? Was the king perhaps seduced by her? Bathsheba, after all, makes an appearance among the ancestors of Jesus in Matthew's genealogy, where she is expressly described as the former wife of Uriah. She is one of the four women, all in various ways ambiguous and surprising presences, who are named in that document. That there was a mystery, a secret, no one could doubt. That the mystery was for the most part to do with the techniques of story-telling rather than with some allegorical message is the modern view I have been describing.

Perhaps this will suffice to show the modern emphasis on the creative character of reading, and on internal relations rather than on historical reference. It has been argued that in the David stories we witness a transition from myth into 'historicized fiction', and there seems no doubt that skills long acquired from the reading of novels can be applied to freshen or even transform our reading of the Bible stories. Such acts of interpretation may be thought of as a modern equivalent to midrash, which, as Rosenberg remarks, knows of no single 'correct' reading, but works to make us suspicious of every detail in the text.

The case is not very different in modern readings of New Testament narrative. They have ancestors, not only Auerbach but Austin Farrer and Amos Wilder. The structure of Mark was long thought to be amenable only to form-critical study; any structure it had was imposed, as it were, from without, in whatever material came into the evangelist's hands. Farrer sought more or less occult indications of interior structuration (Wilder's approach was different). Now books exploring the literary qualities of Mark and the other gospels abound, some on structuralist principles, some using other modern methods or eclectic assemblages of several such, some dealing with isolated passages and some with whole texts. Once again the tendency is to accept the text as we have it rather than to look for a lost text or texts behind it. Narrow notions of intention are eschewed; what matters is that the patterns, analogues, relations, significant silences and significant repetitions are there to be perceived and developed.

This reaction from the 'scientific' scholarly tradition meets, of course, with opposition, some of it very forceful; the new criticism is called a reversion to 'pre-critical' methods. Its practitioners not surprisingly prefer to call their methods, 'post-critical'. Yet it is true that they have some affinities with pre-critical interpretative practices. They require fidelity to the literal but deny that this is a bar to interpretative freedom: so the Tannaim claimed that their *derash* was the true sense of Scripture, and therefore identical with *peshat*, the literal sense; and so medieval Christians held that the literal sense of the Jewish Bible was the sense revealed in the New Testament. Of course the great difference between the old and the new is the difference implied by the term 'historicized fiction'. It took a considerable cultural upheaval to bring on a state of affairs in which it seemed possible, even perhaps necessary, to read the New Testament stories not in order to study their historical reference but to consider them as one might consider other instances of the art of fiction, and to do so in the conviction that this was the way to defend their religious value.

Here are some examples of such readings of Christian narrative. John alone introduces the character of Nicodemus. At his first appearance in chapter 3 Nicodemus seems to be a type-figure, a specimen upper-class Jew, and Jews in John have as their principal function the misunderstanding of Jesus. Nicodemus, 'a ruler of the Jews', well-placed, serious, recognizes that Jesus is 'a teacher come from God'. But we are to infer that this recognition is imperfect because dependent on the miracles ('signs') he has observed – which is the case with most Jewish acknowledgements of Jesus. So his salutation is received not with a courteous word but with a dark saying: 'Except a man be born again, he cannot see the kingdom of God.' Nicodemus is baffled; Jesus, having prefaced his saying with the 'Amen, amen' that vouches for its absolute veracity, has spoken figuratively, and Nicodemus does not understand the figure, blindly supposing that Jesus is talking about carnal generation. His rejoinder produces more gnomic sentences, though by verse 9 he should understand that what is being described is a spiritual rebirth 'from above'. 'How can these things be?' he asks. As so often, Jesus answers the question with another question: 'Art thou a master of Israel, and knowest not these things?' It is as if this intelligent man were missing something obvious. And further explanation, which contains an obscure prophecy of redemption, seems not to help Nicodemus. He does not go out into the night from whence he came; he simply fades away, and the dialogue becomes a monologue. We *could* say, following the critical tradition, that a discourse of Jesus has got attached to a tradition about Nicodemus, or we could hypothesize a careless redactor, who simply forgot to move Nicodemus offstage. Or we could speculate as to what became of him.

He had come in out of the darkness to visit the Light, but he may then have retreated into an even blacker darkness, meriting, therefore, the condemnation of verse 19: 'And this is the condemnation, that light is come into the world, and men loved darkness rather than light, because their deeds were evil'. On the other hand Nicodemus *had* sought the light, and was therefore not one of those who failed to do so lest their deeds should be reproved (verse 20). Some work is here asked of the reader; there is certainly some sort of gap.

It has often been noticed that John likes to make each of his episodes mirror in little the whole narrative, as this one does by prophecy and by implication: the Jews were shown the light but remained dark to the end. But its links with the whole story are too strong to be described as mere reflections or analogues. From the Prologue we know about the cardinal antithesis of darkness and light. We know that in many ways, for example by declaring himself the antitype of Moses lifting up the brazen serpent – 'even so must the Son of man be lifted up' (verse 14) – Jesus affirms a relation of fulfilment to the Old Testament, and the repeated failure of the Jews to understand such typologies is a recurrent theme. So there certainly are reflections. Yet there is something simpler and more striking about the narrative treatment of Nicodemus. He has not in fact disappeared for good. He returns briefly at chapter 7, verse 50. There we learn that some people think of Jesus as 'the Prophet' or 'the Christ', but the Pharisees obstinately declare that people who support him are ignorant of the Law and accursed. They also say that no prophet can come from Galilee. It is at this moment that Nicodemus enquires whether the Law allows a man to be condemned without a hearing, a remark which draws upon him the accusation of being a supporter of Jesus. Nicodemus says only one thing, and it sounds like liberal good sense; but the Pharisees read it as pro-Christian, and they may, by an irony, be right. The implication may be either that proper observance of the Law is in fact Christian; or that Nicodemus is of the Christian party without knowing or openly declaring it. And is he still the puzzled, rational fellow of chapter 3, or does this brief reappearance hint at a development of his capacities?

Another possibility is that John was preparing for the third appearance of Nicodemus at the climax of the story, and, wanting us to keep him in mind, inserted him in the middle as well as at both ends. Yet the final appearance offers no simple and satisfying explanation of his role. It happens at chapter 19, verse 39, when Nicodemus turns up with Joseph of Arimathea, described as a disciple of Jesus; they are bearing ointments to prepare the body for burial. And that is the end of him. We are not told that he had become, or was to become, a disciple. He may simply have wished to honour in death the man he had long since recognized as a great teacher. He may have joined Joseph in order to dissociate himself from the acts and opinions of the Pharisees. If we want to argue that he is no longer among the condemned – or even if we want to argue that he is – we shall have to make up a plot connecting his three appearances, in none of which is he given an unambiguous part to play. John, then, is reticent, he withholds explanations. Narrative certainly serves both to aid memory and to explain; those are its primary functions. But it also deals in oblivion and secrecy.

John is in some ways the most subtle story-teller of the evangelists. The raising of Lazarus is a story told only in his Gospel, and it is quite unlike the raisings from the dead in the others, not least because of its extended treatment and the ambiguities of its presentation. There can be no doubt of its structural significance, occurring as it does at the great hinge of John's narrative, just before the start of the Passion story. Indeed it is more than anything else what makes his account of the last days of Jesus different from all the others. In John, Lazarus is one target of the chief priests' enmity – they rather absurdly want to kill him for having been resurrected and making converts in the process. Some will say that John put the tale together from disparate parts of the other gospels; but however he came by the material he clearly resolved to treat it differently, for example in the matter of length – forty-five verses from the announcement of Lazarus's sickness to his emergence from the tomb.

Jesus announces that the sickness is not unto death; and for reasons we can only guess at he delays for two days his journey to Bethany. At verse 14 he announces plainly that Lazarus is dead, with an implication that he, Jesus, had required this to be the case ('I am glad for your sakes that I was not there, to the intent ye may believe'). Six verses later Martha comes out to meet him, with what sounds like a quiet reproach: 'If thou hadst been here, my brother had not died.' He assures her that her brother will rise from the dead. Martha takes this to mean that he will rise 'at the last day'; and Jesus tells her 'I am the resurrection and the life.' After twelve more verses, Mary, the other sister, encounters Jesus, repeating Martha's complaint almost word for word: 'if thou hadst been here my brother had not died.' We may now have some expectation that Jesus will repeat his words to Martha; instead, he weeps. He shows signs of great distress, 'groaning in himself' (verse 38); and in the account of the dead man's emergence from the tomb it is almost as if Jesus himself were suffering birth-pangs, crying out 'with a loud voice, Lazarus, come forth' (verse 43). And Lazarus does come forth, still bound in his grave clothes.

Why is the conversation with Martha partly, but only partly, repeated with Mary? It is sometimes suggested, in the 'critical' manner, that the author or redactor is clumsily putting together two traditions. That view takes no account of the narrative depth and richness of the passage. The progress of Jesus to the tomb is uncannily slow, as verse 30 emphasizes; it is as if, in the midst of all the interruptions, some ritual were being performed. We expect the meeting with Mary to replicate exactly that with Martha, as it might in a folk-tale (or a rite); perhaps a third encounter will follow, as, with enormous effect, it does, when Lazarus also comes out to meet him. But the meeting with Mary is not a duplicate; there is no repetition of the divine pronouncement ('I am the resurrection and the life' – the *ego eimi*, the 'I am' of John is always an affirmation of divinity). Instead there is a man, weeping, capable of human love and grief. He asks where Lazarus has been laid, and says nothing more until the prayer and the command to come forth, which is uttered in a loud voice – the Greek words being exactly the same as those used by Matthew of Jesus uttering his last cry on the cross, also dying to bring about rebirth.

There is here a blend of reticence and express statement. Martha is played off against Mary, the humanity of Jesus against his divinty; this most spectacular miracle is finally a figure for the spiritual sense of resurrection and its human cost. It has many functions, including a part in the political plot. It remembers the plot of miracle or sign misunderstood. One could go on. But the point is its reticence, and its imaginative resource, not inferior to those of the great Old Testament stories.

One final example: this time a story told by all four evangelists, so that here we have an advantage denied us in the other instances cited, namely that we can see what four different hands made of the same material. The story is of the anointing of Jesus at the house of Lazarus, Martha and Mary in Bethany. At any rate, that is John's story. In Mark and Matthew the anointing is done by a 'woman', not otherwise described or named, at the house of Simon the leper (Mark 14 : 3, Matthew 26 : 6). In both these versions the woman pours the ointment on the head of Jesus; in Mark some, and in Matthew all, of the disciples protest about the waste, and are reproved by Jesus, who says the woman has done a beautiful thing and prepared his body for burial (verses 3–9, 6–13). Luke places the story earlier in the ministry and says that it happened in the house of Simon the *Pharisee*; he describes the woman as a 'sinner' (Luke 7: 35–50). This woman washes the feet of Jesus and wipes them with her hair before anointing his head. The Pharisee says to himself that a genuine prophet would have known the woman was a sinner; and Jesus, reading his thoughts, replies with a parable-like saying that the woman's love is greater than the Pharisee's, and that her sins, though many, will be forgiven.

Obviously Luke's point would have been lost had Simon himself been a leper and so unclean, for he wanted the contrast between the Pharisee and his loveless virtue and the woman sinner with her faith and devotion. Mark had something else in mind, namely Jesus's choice of table companions, and his wish to act as physician to the sick. John deviates even more widely from the Marcan account than Luke does. With his usual economy he identifies the woman with Mary, the sister of Lazarus. She anoints his feet, not his head – and that is an extraordinary thing to have done; she then wipes his feet with her hair, which is even more extraordinary, more appropriate to Luke's sinner than to a virtuous woman. The protest against waste, which is omitted by Luke and in Mark and Matthew made by several disciples or all of them, is made in John's version by Judas alone. John alone characterized Judas as the thieving purse-bearer, now ripe for an act much more wicked than petty theft. His complaint is preceded by a clear indication of its place in his developing career as a criminal: 'Then saith one of the disciples, Judas Iscariot, Simon's son, which should betray him' (John 12 : 4).

John's version exhibits a concern for causal connection and economy of characterization that is found everywhere in his narrative. Some might prefer Luke's version, which is adorned by a parable and contains a well-wrought contrast between the reserve of the Pharisee and the tenderness of the woman. But John has found a stronger place for the tale; he relates it not only to the coming betrayal but to the earlier scene with Mary before the raising of Lazarus. It is interesting that this tradition of interpretation by narrative (clearly originating in the 'midrashic habit') should have been continued in later Christian thought; for the woman not otherwise specified by Mark and Matthew, and the woman who was in Luke a sinner, and Mary, the sister of Lazarus in John, were combined with Mary Magdalen not only in the popular imagination, but also in the ecclesiastic tradition, for the identification is perpetuated in the Roman Catholic liturgical calendar.

When one speaks of connexity in New Testament narratives one should not neglect the deepest connection of all, the connection with the Jewish Bible. I cannot now enlarge on that theme – the creation of fictive history or historicized fiction by the development of ancient narrative germs. It is a dominant characteristic of New Testament narrative. To rewrite the old in terms of a later state of affairs is an ancient Jewish practice. One of the points I have tried to make is that in their manner of writing stories there was much in common between the authors of the two Bibles. A re-evaluation of their techniques and methods in the light of our own knowledge of what it is to follow – to co-operate with – a story should serve to refresh our perceptions. And it may not be too much to hope that the efforts now being devoted to this end may solve some of the difficulties that have for so long beset modern readers of ancient writings.

NOTES

1 James S. Ackerman, 'Joseph, Judah and Jacob', in Kenneth R. R. Gros Louis and J. S. Ackerman (eds), *More Literary Interpretations of Biblical Narratives* (Nashville: Abingdon, 1982).
2 Tzvetan Todorov, *The Poetics of Prose*, trans. Richard Howard (Ithaca, NY, 1977) pp. 53–65; Robert Alter, *The Art of Biblical*

Narrative (New York: Basic Books, 1981) p. 21.

3 Frank MacShane (ed.), *Ford Madox Ford: The Critical Heritage* (London: Routledge, 1972) pp. 47–51.

4 'The Challenge of the Texts', Commencement Address at the Los Angeles School, Hebrew Union College, 1985.

5 Robert Alter, *The Art of Biblical Narrative* (New York: Basic Books, 1981) p. 182.

6 Adele Berlin, *Poetics and Interpretation of Biblical Narrative* (Sheffield: Sheffield University Press, 1983) pp. 26–7.

7 Joel Rosenberg, 'Meanings, Morals and Mysteries: Literary Approaches to Torah', *Response*, no. 26 (1975) 67ff.

Poetry and History

It seems that more and more people are turning away from the idea that literary works should be treated as autonomous and without significant relation to the world in which they are produced and read. It is even one of the charges against the influential practitioners of deconstruction that they have sealed off the text from the social context. Those who are anxious to establish, or re-establish, the relation or dialogue between literature and history differ in many respects, but feminism, neo-Marxism and neo-historicism are alike in this concern for non-literary contexts. It can take pretty tortuous forms, but when Terry Eagleton, for instance, talks about the 'complex series of transactions between text and ideology which are concealed by the apparent concreteness and naturalness of the text' he is of course speaking as a Marxist, but with small alteration the words might well be used by feminists.[1]

All such talk presupposes something like a determinate and intelligible status for history; and those responsible would doubtless have little time for Karl Popper's opinion: 'Although history has no meaning, we can give it a meaning.'[2] But of course we also inherit and endorse or qualify meanings given by others, and the written history on which speculation of this sort must depend may itself be thought of as a kind of imaginative fiction, or a poem, persuasive, ordered, endowed with at least the simulacra of causality, and of course the record, already established, of complex transaction with ideologies.

Thinking of history in that light, we can try to say something about its relations with poetry which evades the ideologies brought to it, *a priori*, by Marxists or feminists; not with the intention of showing them to be wrong, but to stress the legitimate possibility of variety. And to simplify the task we may speak only of a limited type of history, the sort that makes the past easier to deal with by punctuating the record with great crises and great persons. This is a variety of history with obvious mnemonic attractions; it is also in some measure shared by all, learned and simple alike, even in this critical age. It might be called history as myth, or as poem. In fact I shall talk about the relation of such poems to the poems written about them, in celebration of the great events given historical centrality by communal acts of historical imagination. This modest enterprise, I should add, may be seen as an archaism, a reversion to a mode of literary history now finally discredited. But I offer no apology, since something of the kind must happen if we are not to collude with the destruction of certain values not easily attained but too easily lost.

A vast number of poems have been written in celebration of historical events, from great victories to royal birthays, and on the whole we pay them little attention. One reason may be that many such poems simply comply with their occasions, and pass into oblivion with those occasions. At any rate it can be argued that the poems about history we continue to value tend to be complicated, ambiguous, and if only in that respect deviant from any official and any popular view of their occasions. I shall try to show that this is true of three such poems, widely separated in time, and hope you will infer that it is likely to be true of any others one might reasonably introduce into the discussion.

The three poems are Horace's 'Actium Ode' (III.37),

Marvell's 'Horatian Ode on Cromwell's Return from Irleand' and Auden's poem 'Spain, 1937'.

Nunc est bibendum

Forsan et haec olim meminisse iuvabit, as people used to say in the school magazine. Why was I, aged fifteen, required to sit in a provincial schoolroom, chanting *nunc est bidendum?* The Latin was difficult, and we had no natural concern with Alcaic metre or the battle of Actium. Nor did anybody seriously attempt to explain why we should develop such a concern. But we were at a *grammar* school, and grammar still meant Latin. Ours was the tribute of the vulgar to the *grammatica*, the old imperial speech of Rome, which, unlike our barbaric tongues, was immutable. We were still discharging a debt contracted when the Romans were kind enough to invade us.

That Latin was good for our careers, and good for us, was an assumption hardly to be questioned, nor was it necessary to explain the myth on which it was based, a myth the more powerful because not recognized as a myth. And so we were obliged to discover what Horace had to say about his world-historical emperor and his world-changing victory in Egypt; and also to investigate his achievement in the naturalization of Greek metres, and the exploitation of the delicacy and strength of his dialect, which was the language of the centre, of power and luxury and the only history that really counted.

Much of this mythology is now dead, though there is still a sense, rather tenuous, that we belong to the *imperium* inaugurated by Augustus at the great turn of time, at Actium. We may still, then, have some interest in what Horace says about the myth at its moment of origin, the moment at which the poem of history is not only formed but breeds deviant versions.

The battle was fought in 31 BC. The defeat of Antony

and Cleopatra meant that the Roman Empire would face westward, that its metropolis would stand on the Tiber rather than the Nile, that *virtus* would be the ethical norm rather than *voluptas*, and so forth. This we know not only from the historians but from Shakespeare. We also know of a further providential arrangement, whereby, following Actium, there was an Augustan Peace, ensuring suitable conditions for the birth of Christ, Actium, in short, was truly decisive. Pascal was serious when he remarked that if Cleopatra's nose had been shorter the whole face of the world would have changed.

What the historians tell us in addition is that Octavius prepared for a definitive contest with Antony, though he declared war only on Cleopatra, thus ensuring that the war was not technically a civil war; Antony was treated as one who had made common cause with the nation's enemies. After the victory Octavius closed the Temple of Janus and inaugurated an imperial peace. Poets joined him in celebrating the traditional republican virtues, glossing over his assumption of unprecedented powers. He became divine. He was certainly, if the expression means anything, a great man. Actium may not have been much of a battle, as battles go, but even the most sober historian concurs, in his or her own style, with the legend: it could be said to have changed the course of history.

So it was worth celebrating. Cleopatra was feared and despised; an imperial rival, she threatened Rome with oriental barbarism. It was best not to name her: the hated word *regina* was enough, and that is all Horace calls her. Antony he does not mention at all. He gets details of the battle wrong, saying, for example, that the queen escaped with barely one ship (she had sixty), affirming incorrectly that Octavius himself pursued her. He ignores the fact that the Egyptian campaign did not end at Actium, though it is true that it was good as over when Antony removed himself from the scene. And sober historians suggest that Horace (like Plutarch and Shakespeare after him) was wrong in supposing that Octavius really wanted Cleopatra in his triumph. He was smart enough to see that she was much better dead, and took no excessive precautions to prevent her suicide. Indeed it is not certain that she did kill herself; the asps – Egyptian cobras, which kill painlessly – were sometimes used by assassins. It is occasionally hinted that Octavius actually had her murdered.

However, Horace (though some suppose him to have been present at the battle) prefers, to this extent at any rate, the myth to the facts. Let us, for convenience have an inadequate summary of his poem:

Now we have proper cause for celebration – hitherto it would have been wrong to drink the ancestral wine, for the state was under threat from Cleopatra and her depraved company. Her drunken fantasies of conquest evaporated when Caesar defeated her, pursuing her like a hunter. Accepting the fact of disaster, she drank and with her body the serpent's venom; no humble woman, she declined to be taken to Rome and displayed in a triumph.

Even from this very inadequate account it is possible to see how the tone of the poem changes, beginning with exultation in victory and ending with a tribute to a courage above the 'womanly'. The change comes when Caesar destroys her fantasies and forces her to contemplate the terrors of reality (*redegit in veros timores*). After that the note of respect is only partly grudging. She is *deliberata morte ferocior*, fiercer in her premeditated death; she is *non humilis mulier*, a woman by no means base or ignoble. And perhaps in the hunting figures used of Caesar's pursuit one can even hear a faint undertone of contempt: the hawk chases the dove, the hunter the hare, yet Cleopatra is not that kind of quarry: *fatale mostrum*, dreadful prodigy, hardly dove or hare; *generosius* suggests an aristocratic fineness in the acceptance of a death apparently coarse (*asperas . . . serpentes*).

The commentators not only point out historical inaccuracies, foreshortenings and so on but occasionally pass a moral judgement, as when the simile of hawk and dove is said to be lacking 'in both truth and humanity', and *remis adurgens* misleading;[3] or when Fraenkel commends the magnanimity of the poem as well as praising the 'architecture' of the concluding sentence.[4] But commentators who concern themselves with the ripples and intricate tidal movements of the piece are rarer. One such is Steele Commager, who notes that drinking provides the 'articulating image' of the poem: there is a pun on *libero* in the first line (Liber is Bacchus); they drink Caecuban wine; Cleopatra is *fortuna . . . dulci ebria*, which literally recalls her carousing, and figuratively the source of her ambition. Before. Actium she was drunk with power (*dementis, inpotens, furorem* and so on) and her final drink also 'hovers between the literal and the figurative' – *conbiberet venenum*. Drunken irresponsibility, says Commager, gives way to a higher freedom. The ode has a 'double moral commitment', and its poetic intentions cross at the moment of the hunting similes, which are better suited to pity than fear; Caesar as hawk and hunter of hares is anyway not very glorious, and our sympathies swing away from him and stay with Cleopatra. So a song of triumph 'slides into . . . a panegyric of the vanquished queen, serene of countenance, *voltu sereno*'.[5]

We now see that anything like strict attention to the language of the poem at once leads the critic away from the simple historical record, and the simple historical myth. If you want to explain away the poem's apparent self-contradictions you can argue that by exalting Cleopatra in this way – making her heroic and maintaining that she had a terrible grandeur in defeat – Horace was cunningly emphasizing the size of the Roman achievement in getting rid of her. You must, perhaps, choose between that explanation and some other, more generous, which also takes account of the way in which the poem subverts its ostensible theme and mood. It winds through its narrow channels of metre and stanza, varied, sinuous, in its last tortuous sentence deferring yet tending towards its unforeseeable climax, *non humilis mulier triumpho*, where, as Commager remarks, '*Superbo* and *non humilis* are practically identical, and as we read the last line it is easy to forget that *mulier* and *triumpho* are logically opposed. The verbal arrangement suggests that the triumph belongs to Cleopatra as well' (p. 93). Some of the glory of Caesar is forfeit to the humbled who yet refused humility. There can, in such a poem, be no straight run of argument, for its own figures, its own syntax, continually distract it; what ends at the end is the simplicity of the myth with which, at the outset, the poem seemed to comply. In the light of that poem the myth casts a shadow, an image not of public rejoining but of something more private and more complex, resistant to communal simplicities. And this, rather than some plain record of popular pleasure, is what we choose to preserve.

'Tis time to leave the books in dust

In the early summer of 1650 Marvell wrote his poem about the historical crisis only just past, or perhaps still in progress. It was of a lesser scale than Horace's, or most people would say so; yet it was in some respects parallel to it. At the end of January 1647, Charles I became the prisoner of Parliament. Entrusted to the care of the army, he escaped and fled to the Isle of Wight. A Scottish force which crossed the border to support him was defeated by Cromwell at Preston in the summer of 1648. After the purging of a hundred members thought likely to oppose such a course, Parliament constituted a court to try the king on an unprecedented charge: treason to the Commonwealth of England. He was found guilty and executed on 30 January 1649. Cromwell then 'pacified'

Ireland in a ferocious campaign, and shortly afterwards –
Marvell's poem was written in the interval – invaded
Scotland, where Charles II had been recognized as king.
Cromwell was technically the instrument of Parliament,
but before long he was for all practical purposes a king
himself, and in 1653 was named Lord Protector.

Marvell does not discuss in any particular way the rights
and wrongs and purposes of the Civil War which resulted
in the death of the king. He will not, in this poem, have
anything relevant to say about issues which later interested
historians, such as the transfer of power from a would-be
absolutist monarchy to the landed gentry. He is interested
in politics of a higher, perhaps one could even say more
mythical, cast. The Stuarts claimed divine right, and
Charles I had done so with great emphasis and assurance,
governing for years without a parliament. Propaganda of
fantastic elaboration and persistence had reinforced these
claims. One element in the propaganda was the inheritance
by English kings of the Roman *imperium*, the line running
from Augustus (victor of Actium) through the first Christian
(and half-English) emperor Constantine. When Marvell
speaks of 'the antient rights' he may have in mind
the English constitution (though Charles's attitude to
parliaments may be thought at odds with that concept)
but was surely thinking also of this imperial myth,
assiduously cultivated by the Stuarts in the masques
performed in that very Banqueting House, built by Inigo
Jones for Charles's father James I, outside which the
Committee for the King's Execution set up their scaffold.
The choice of site was not accidental, and we need not
think its significance was lost on Marvell.

We can see that his decision to take the political ode of
Horace as his model was very apt. In a sense he is
celebrating the end of an epoch that began with the victory
at Actium. Since English did not accept quantitative verse
he invented an English stanza that recalls the alcaics of
Horace – a four-lined stanza with two rhymed couplets,

the second set off from the first, trimeters against tetrameters. The rhymes, close together in the second couplet, give the English stanza an Horatian resistance to the forward movement of the sentences; for the syntactic complexities of the Latin are substituted the semantic complexities – the puns and ambiguities – of the English. The best parallel I can think of is the pseudo-*terza rima* of Eliot's 'Little Gidding', where the decision was *not* to rhyme, because rhyme in English cannot be as unobtrusive as rhyme in Italian; and Eliot, by judicious use of feminine endings mixed with masculine, is alone among English translators and imitators in reproducing something like the distinctive gait of Dante.

Consequently, just as Eliot's lines exist, so to speak, in the aural shadow of Dante, so Marvell's ode on the end of the ancient *imperium* is intimate with Horace's celebration of its beginning (though it remembers other ancient sources as well). And in its handling of the myth of the great event, its deviations and shifts of emphasis, it again resembles Horace. We know that royalists at first took it for a royalist poem and circulated it surreptitiously; we also know that it was deleted from the posthumous first edition of Marvell's poems in 1681, presumably because later Stuart eyes read it as Cromwellian. There are other reasons for thinking Marvell's own political position in 1650 obscure; all we need to say now is that his poem does not obviously comply with any popular or partisan view of its occasion. And it is in the veiled quality of the work, the tones seemingly so unillusioned and, at least at moments, decided, yet resonant of indecision and mystery, that we might think its greatness lies.

'Caesar' is a central figure in Marvell as well as in Horace, but in Marvell his head is blasted by a force as irresistible as lightning, lightning which has first shattered the force of its own 'side' before acting like providence – 'the force of angry heaven's flame' – so that Cromwell becomes one of those world-historical figures whose acts are in the service of a higher power. But are we simply to accept this version of events? Are we being told that all resistance to the forces of history are vain? Certainly the poem seems to be saying so, and it continues in a deliberative, concessive tone, as if praising Cromwell with no more than the proper measure of approval: after all, even if the bit about the lightning and the laurels may sound a bit excessive, surely this man deserves credit, having emerged from rural obscurity, and by labour and valour climbed – to what? To political eminence? No: but 'to ruin the great work of time', so reversing the usual arrangements, whereby time ruins the great works of men. Cromwell melts down the old constitution like a ruined bell, and makes a new one in another mould. The sequence is Horatian; it moves, in a sentence, from the judicious award of credit to Cromwell ('And, if we would speak true, / Much to the man is due') through his private garden, in which, though austere, his work is of small import, a prettiness almost ('As if his highest plot / To plant the bergamot') to the vast claims that follow, the destruction and renovation of the state. And in their turn these claims are undercut by the reasonable, pseudo-Machiavellian progress of the argument:

> Though Justice against Fate complain,
> And plead the antient rights in vain;
>   But those do hold or break
>   As men are strong or weak.

Here we have an apparently direct reply to the words spoken by the king at his trial, for he asked how any citizen could call his life and possessions his own 'if power without right daily make new, and abrogate the fundamental laws of the land'.[6] This seemingly straightforward political expression is, however, complicated by the pseudo-scientific figures of penetration and vacuum, which we can take as we like, as argument for or against Cromwell's status as a 'greater spirit'.

The passage on the arrest and execution of the king stretches from line 49 to line 72, in a poem of 120 lines spanning its central section and suggesting that the real centre is here, at the moment when the ancient rights are extinguished. This set-piece, however, is introduced by way of praising Cromwell's 'art'. Here is a king on a scaffold such as might be used by street players, though built on to the very room where the Royal Actor played out his scenes on the stages and with the courtly machinery and costumes of Inigo Jones. Now his art is to be exercised in another purpose-built theatre, this time not to aggrandize but to destroy him. He is an actor, of course, in another sense: this is his last act. The literal and figurative senses are inextricable. The scaffold is doubly tragic – it will represent the death of a great man by the death of a great man. He gives a good performance, he 'adorns' the stage; the verb is associated with the performances of actors ('a new Cibber might the stage adorn', *Dunciad*, iii. 134). The armed bands are clapping like an audience (though it is said the purpose was to drown out the hero's dying speech). The performance made the *scene* memorable – 'scene' in the theatrical sense, and also in its usual transferred and commonplace sense (the *OED* confirms the intermingling of these senses at the time); there is a hint that to be a king at all, or even a great man, is to give a performance, to adorn a stage, to be always, in and out of the Banqueting House, on or in a scene.

The protracted obliquity of all this makes even more striking the sudden change from the pathos of 'helpless right' to the drum-roll of the sequel: what was *truly* memorable about that hour (the temporal word replacing 'scene' when its work was done) was after all not the king's performance but the assuring of 'the forced power', and again we have the language of the orator advocating political realism, demanding acknowledgement that rights are upheld by the strength of men, rather than by Banqueting House magic. This affirmation, at first naked, is then enforced by an extraordinary and accurate figure: the discovery by the Roman architects of the bleeding head was at first shocking, but it ensured the future security of the state.

We notice the depth of this calculated analogy: the Rome whose future was secured by the bleeding head of Charles must be a new Rome, a new style of *imperium*. What must follow? Conquest and violent pacification, the achievements of a new Caesar. Perhaps Marvell recalled Horace's Caesar – the hawk pursuing the dove – when he compared Cromwell to a (submissive) falcon; and when he calls him a hunter in cold Caledonia, as Horace makes Caesar hunt the hare across frozen fields. And then he calls Cromwell 'a Caesar'; though he also calls him a Hannibal, and Hannibal was an enemy. He is a Caesar under the new, realistic dispensation; new, though the wisdom that informs it is as old as Sallust: 'the same arts that did gain / A power must it maintain.'

So Marvell, like Horace, celebrates the great event in what is ostensibly a decisive manner; and possibly one can explain the fluctuations of tone as merely the tactics of skilful oratory, concessions to the opposite view being there only to be cancelled, ancient rights given a value only by way of explaining the necessity of their overthrow. Just so, some maintain, Horace praised Cleopatra merely for tactical reasons. On the other hand the praise of Cromwell has a distinctly uncertain tonality. He is a kind of Scipio, looking after his garden, reserved and austere, until called to save the state. He is a natural force like thunder, king-killing thunder. He is a great spirit and a crafty regicide; an obedient falcon, a ruthless deer-hunter; perhaps, in the last lines, an Aeneas (founder of the state) drawing his sword against phantoms. He is what on some views a great man needs to be, ruthless, committed to conquest; while the king, who was weak and who broke, compels a (perhaps discardable) admiration.

The poem winds itself in and out of these attitudes, its figuration often centripetal in respect of the ostensible theme; if it is deliberative, it also ironized its deliberations. It does not weigh the evidence like a newspaper leader which knows what side it will end on; it does not put the case for the beauty of an *ancien régime* like, say, Burke on Marie Antoinette; but it does not, either, speak for Fate against Justice, or for a Machiavellian *virtù*. It will not submit to doctrine or myth; its light strikes the myth and casts another shadow. If it were simply the cry of a public occasion we should long since have forgotten it and ceased to offer interpretations (as the bibliographies show we certainly have not). It is in the nature of the case that the simplicities of somebody else's remote celebration do not interest us, caught in our own moment, and with our own ideas of what makes poems and history interesting; and that is always language, and language to some degree private, observing but also flouting ordinary usage, alive therefore with shifting senses, with figures also that shift between the impossible literal and the boundless figurative.

Today the Struggle

Auden's poem offers a different perspective on our problem. The civil war in Spain certainly seemed to be an event of critical importance, whichever side one was on. The poem was published in May 1937 as a pamphlet in support of Medical Aid for Spain. The poet had recently returned to England from Valencia and Barcelona, where he had done some propaganda for the Republican side. The red cover of the pamphlet is a fair indication of his political sympathies; at the time he was quite explicitly pro-communist and anti-fascist, and like many others he thought Spain was the right place and moment to make a stand. But he had disliked much of what he saw of Republican behaviour.

The poem is notorious for the complexity of interpretation it has provoked, not least in the poet himself, who revised it, then condemned it as false, and finally excluded it from the canon of his work.

His doubts have often been echoed. Later attitudes to that war are not likely to be less ambivalent than those of the thirties; the simplicity of myth – the conviction that the Spanish Republic could, by defeating fascism, have inaugurated a new epoch in world history – are no longer available; simply, too much is known. The diagrammatic or mythical view of the matter which sent volunteers by the thousand to fight before Madrid is lost for ever.

But Auden's poem does not offer such a view; and in so far as it is the work of a poet intoxicated by the huge resources of language, the inexhaustible treasury of fact and figure given relevance by their associations in his own mind, it could not do so. Edward Mendelson, Auden's most authoritative commentator, calls 'Spain' 'an extraordinarily complex poem' and regards it as 'the record of a disillusionment half-accepted, half-denied. Auden asserts that a certain form of partisan political action can express the will of love and foster ultimate justice; but he also knows that the political action today claiming to express these things in fact does nothing of the kind'. And Mendelson then tells us of the poet's own later reaction to the poem – his horror that in his account of the action of history he has equated 'goodness with success' (a criticism that could, with as much justice, be made of Marvell's Ode). Mendelson thinks Auden had a right to say that the last two lines embody 'a wicked doctrine'. But he admits that critics have an equal right to find in those lines merely an extension of 'a quite innocuous argument made earlier in the poem to the effect that history is the product of human choices, and . . . that once these choices are made they cannot be altered, that if we fail to act now, we shall get no second chance'.

So the poem is divided against itself. Its manifest argument says that humans, unlike the shark or the robin, must make their own choices and live with the futures they create. But the metaphoric argument fights against the manifest. The manifest argument speaks of the volunteers as men who made their conscious choice to fight in Spain; but the figures describing their journeys to Spain compare them to gulls, seeds, burrs, clouds, flotsam:

> having been told by 'the life' that they are forever separated from the unthinking processes of nature, [they] immediately became part of those processes by going to Spain. . . . So while the poem's manifest argument maintains that all human actions are chosen by the will, the metaphoric argument maintains that some special actions in the political realm, actions directed at certain social goals, are the product not of will but of something very much like instinctive nature.[7]

This is judicious and sensitive, but it errs in treating the conflict between 'manifest' and 'metaphoric' as the direct reflection of an intellectual confusion on the part of the poet. In so far as it speaks of a confrontation between an hypostasized History and a collection of fugitive, subversive, figures, it is right. We easily think of History not as a record but as a force, and it is roughly the force Marvell called 'Fate'. That is why Auden personifies History, as he does Life. The manifest argument is itself, to this extent, figurative. The moral is much the same as Marvell's: 'These do hold or break / As men are strong or weak', but tonal variation and metaphor are always dragging the argument away from such simple and 'manifest' declarations.

Auden's way of suggesting the coincidence of the poem and the crucial historical moment is to sketch a yesterday and a tomorrow, with 'today' in between: 'today the struggle'. 'Struggle' was a loaded word at the time, for it meant the fight against capitalism; but its sense widens, and it connotes also the moral choices which, as the poem insists, are the privilege or burden of the human animal alone. 'Yesterday' is conveyed with a sort of knowing but random specificity, what Mendelson compactly calls a 'grand synecdochal panorama' (p. 316) – 'the diffusion / Of the counting-frame and the cromlech . . . the assessment of insurance by cards . . . the invention / Of cartwheels and clocks' – all discoveries that travelled slowly along the trade routes, all amazing, yet in their very diffuseness irrelevant to the present moment, in which the Struggle subsumes all other effort. The characteristic 'Audenesque' sprinkling of definite articles is a period mannerism no longer much to our taste, but effective in this context; bizarre as the chosen details may be, you are expected to take from their very oddity and dispersion the hint that in a full account they would be innumerable, whereas there is, today, need for only one slogan, the struggle.

That slogan is thrice repeated before anything else that is contemporary appears in the poem. Then there enter three type figures – 'the poet', 'the investigator' and 'the poor' – all doing and saying unexpected, elliptical things, though with the appeal of the poor to History we are on the point of arriving at the central theme; History and 'The Life', to which the nations appeal in chorus, are really the same, and what they say is that men are not like the other animals; that History and Life will not act for them. '. . . the life, if it answers at all, replies . . . I am whatever you do' – however trivial and selfish and comfortable, however grand, joking in bars or building the Just City. And the Life which is thus 'your choice, your decision', suddenly shifts its name and shape: 'I am Spain'.

This brilliant rhetorical move ensures that what now calls the volunteers to Spain, the men who made their choice for the Just City, who 'came to present their lives', are summoned by a Spain which is somehow identical with life under threat – life, but also the diagram and fever chart of all the illnesses that threaten life and can be cured only by the right choice. For the sake of this single-minded act the future, like the past must be neglected; there it is, in its random seriousness and possible innocence, to be driven out of mind by the slogan of today. The choice of today, as we now learn, entails the guilt, tedium and hardship of war. It entails also the loneliness of the person who chooses such things. The animals are unconcerned, history will not help; 'we are left alone with our day'.

And then comes that famous last stanza, which the poet himself so detested. 'It would be bad enough if I had ever held this wicked doctrine, but that I should have stated it simply because it sounded to me rhetorically effective is quite inexcusable'[8] Yet, like the rest of the poem, these lines concern the solitariness of the human chooser, and the urgency of his choice:

> The stars are dead; the animals will not look:
> We are left alone with our day, and the time is
> short and
> History to the defeated
> May say Alas but cannot help or pardon.

Not for the first time one feels that Auden willed himself into misunderstanding his own poems when he changed his politics and developed a new aesthetic that refused to distinguish poems from lies. What the personified History says is another piece of ancient wisdom, like 'The same arts that did gain / A power must it maintain.' It says: the choice is yours, you must make it now; if you fail I shall be sorry, but have no power to console or absolve. Auden seems to have regarded this – and the whole poem – as the false expression of a polarized political attitude; but in doing so he was surely wrong. Leaving aside the issue of the last lines (it is of course possible to disagree with the sentiment, as it is with Marvell's), the entire poem cannot avoid the diffusion of sense and figure upon which its whole rhetoric insists; as it concentrates upon its moment it also scatters attention from it, with its fairies and gargoyles, pageants and bicycle-races. The mistake is simply to suppose that it *can*, in these terms, be saying one thing only, whether one applauds or deplores that one thing.

Indeed, that is why it is valuable as a poem; it is too good to comply with its moment or its myth. It confounds or beautifully smudges their clarity; much as Horace and Marvell had done when they contemplated Rome and England in their vast and obvious crises.

Poetry and History

Although the categories are never quite distinct, we know in general the differences between historical record, historical myth and historical poem. We are ready to accept, sometimes with a measure of disagreement but more often quite spontaneously, concepts such as the decisive battle, the world-historical individual; we are in need of mnemonics, simplifications, if we are to hold in our minds a past we can contemplate or use. We know that there must be distortions, the distortions inseparable from the application of language to event; and such distortions become an obvious target for the ironies of further critical discourse. Among these, of necessity, we must count such poems as are not (because they cannot be) either record or mythography. If they carry messages about history they do so in a medium which diffuses or ironizes the messages; in so far as we attend to them as poems; in so far as we do not rewrite them in our heads (as Auden rewrote 'Spain') for the sake of discovering something to hate or love or simply to remember, we find ambiguities and contradictions. But we know – are culturally predisposed to know – that this is not the way to read poetry. We know that we have to read it against the grain of the manifest, and because of that requirement *good* poems about historical crises speak a different language from historical record and historical myth. Poems we judge not to be good will usually be poems which quickly sank into one or the other. The poems I have discussed here have not done so, whether we care much or little about the record of myth of the crises they celebrate. They make history strange and they are very private in their handling of the public themes. They can protect us from the familiar; they stand apart from opinion; they are a form of knowledge. Quite simply they are better poems than the myths provide, and much harder to interpret. Which is why the interaction between them and their historical contexts is a subject calling for sublety and caution.

REFERENCES

1 Terry Eagleton, *Criticism and Ideology* (London: Verso, 1976) p. 101.
2 Karl Popper, *The Open Society and its Enemies*, first published 1945 (London: Routledge & Kegan Paul, 1962) p. ii. 278.
3 R. G. M. Nisbett and M. Hubbard, *A Commentary on the Odes of Horace*, Book I (London: Oxford University Press, 1970) p. 408.
4 E. Fraenkel, *Horace* (London: Oxford University Press, 1957) p. 160.
5 Steele Commager, *The Odes of Horace* (New Haven: Yale University Press, 1962) pp. 88ff.
6 *The Letters and Speeches of Oliver Cromwell*, ed. W. C. Abbott (Cambridge, Mass.: Harvard University Press, 1937) p. i. 738.
7 *Early Auden* (London: Faber, 1981) pp. 315–19.
8 Foreword to *Collected Shorter Poems* (New York: Random House, 1966).

Traditions and Literary Studies: An Interview with Frank Kermode

PAYNE   In your first Lord Northcliffe Lecture, published in *History and Value*, you pick up several subjects about which you've written quite extensively. You spoke about pastoralism, about Lawrence, Eliot and Stevens, and also about the Book of Revelation. Is there a thread that, for you, runs through these items of interest? Is there an encompassing theory of literature that you've been working away at?

KERMODE   Well, I think one sees these threads, or perhaps the thread, by hindsight. I often find when I think I've done something – developed a new interest, worked at it a bit and written it out – I find I am, if not repeating myself, at least in an area where I've been before without realizing that I'd gone back there. So I think one has inherent limitations of interest and that probably they get narrower as one gets older. This time, for instance, in the lectures that I have been giving in Oxford and London, I thought, as I've been working for some years now quite close to biblical studies, I would make a clean break. In the 1930s I was ten when they began and twenty when they ended, and I read a lot of books towards the end of that period. I thought I would look at them again and have a kind of binocular vision of the literature in the thirties, in fact a clean break from everything I've been doing for the last few years. Well, I did that, and now, of course, I find as you've suggested, in the course of doing so, all sorts of King Charles's heads pop out. And so, I think it is true that you might think you're making a great leap, but the leap is confined by your own limitations to quite a small one in the end. So these lectures turn out to be not on the same line as a lot of other ones that I've given, but at least recognizably from the same limited head.

PAYNE Your work in biblical studies obviously connects with your interest in theory of fiction, and you emphasize that connection in *The Genesis of Secrecy*. Literary Biblical studies is also a topic of great interest among other major literary critics at the present time. How do you account for this interest?

KERMODE Yes, it's peculiar, this sudden desire to take the Bible back and bring it within the purview of secular critics and secular readers. I think it's a good thing. My own coming into it looked accidental, as these things often do. I, of course, had been interested, as you've hinted, in apocalyptic thought, but when I went to Cambridge about twelve or thirteen years ago I was living in college for a while and I found that this left me with an awful lot of time in the evenings; if I had been in London, a lot of it would have gone on other things. And I took up an old resolution that I would one day try to read the Gospels in the original Greek. But my Greek was very rusty by this time. So I did buy a couple of New Testament Greek handbooks, primers, and I set myself to learn enough Greek to read the Gospels, which I did. And I was like Oscar Wilde who, when he was examined at Oxford, found them very interesting because it was the stories he was reading. He had to translate from the Greek during his examinations, and they said, well, that's quite enough Mr Wilde. And he said, oh, but do let me go on, I want to see what happens. Well, I was a bit like that really. I did get very interested in the stories, and then of course I saw, which is perfectly obvious to anybody, that these are narratives like any other narratives and that they are subject to the same constraints. The whole question of the relationship between fictive narrative and historical narrative is clearly involved in the structure of the Gospels and the generic problems which they raise. All these things came into my mind when I was thinking about them, including, of course, the special literary problems that they have, like the relationship between the three synoptic Gospels and the relative independence of John, and the quite individual structure of the fourth Gospel. All those things I applied myself to, really with such equipment as I already had plus what I'd picked up by trying to familiarize myself with some of the latest biblical scholarship. So that's how *The Genesis of Secrecy* came to be, as it was then that I was asked to give those lectures at Harvard. I think they give you about eighteen months notice; during the waiting period, of course, I was busy teaching and so on. In the end, when you're asked to do something like that you have to do it on something that's in your head then, and you can't later decide to do something else. So that's how I came to choose the subject of *The Genesis of Secrecy* lectures.

PAYNE One of the things that first struck me when I read *The Genesis of Secrecy*, which seemed unique among the literary critical books I knew on the Bible, was the great respect that you have for traditional biblical scholarship. There's an attitude that runs from Moulton to perhaps Helen Gardner, that if a literary critic has a weekend free, he or she can perhaps straighten out problems in biblical studies that fusty scholars have not been able to work through. But that's not at all the case with your book. You pick up on the traditions of biblical scholarship and weave those, as I read you in that book, into a consideration of the structures of narrative in which contemporary fiction and biblical texts meet.

KERMODE   I think you're right. There are two things to be said about that. One is that the professional quality of much technical biblical scholarship is very high; I think far higher than we're normally accustomed to in our profession. You can't really help being struck by that. And since these texts have been minutely examined for a very long time, that scholarship has created a very powerful tradition. That tradition has its bad side as well as its good, I think, and this is my second point. The training that, until quite recently, people have had in biblical scholarship was immensely thorough. For instance, they know a great deal more Greek than most people who aren't biblical scholars, and they have Hebrew and Aramaic and many other things, a lack of which handicaps the non-professional. The force of that tradition has another effect, and that is that it's very hard to look outside it. People get trapped in it, and ever since the Enlightenment, I suppose, you could say that the main business of technical biblical scholarship has been to break down the books from what they are into what they may have been at some time in the past. This is explained, very reasonably, by the importance which people attach to what's in the books rather than to the books themselves, to the message rather than the medium; and so they try to find what lay behind the text they have before it was redacted. They want to get back as close as possible to the original event or the original person who is being talked about in the books. That is why the tradition contained all these very elaborate hypotheses about documents which preceded the documents that we have, about redactors of different sorts whose works were combined, with all kinds of consequential errors (or what appear to be errors), overlaps, repetitions and all the rest of it. That tradition, which is very subtle, has really made it difficult over the years for people who work in it to think of these books as wholes. Now the justification of thinking of them as complete and whole in themselves, the historical justification is really very strong. That is the way they have been looked at for a very long time.

Let's give an example, the Gospel of Matthew, for instance. For a hundred odd years, although it's been challenged recently, the view has been that Matthew is conflated from Mark plus another lost document called 'Q', and possibly something else as well. Scholars attempt to reconstruct 'Q', which may never have existed, but if it did exist it has long since been caught up into Matthew and Luke. And that's all we know about it, from traces in Matthew and Luke. If you concentrate then on what lay behind, you forget that what we think of as the Gospel of Matthew, from the time the Gospel of Matthew first existed, has always been a blend of these books, as all books are blends of other books. So there is a real case for taking the thing as it stands. There's a very good example of this in the fourth Gospel, I think, which is the only one that begins with a sort of hymn or prologue, and that prologue has been endlessly disintegrated by technical scholarship. It *is* rather strange, because it seems to end, and then the narrative seems to begin, and then the hymn starts again, and the narrative intrudes. And so a lot of trouble is taken not only to take out the bits that shouldn't be there, but also to show that the theology of the prologue is not the same as that of the Gospels, that very likely what happened was that somebody stuck this hymn on the top of the gospel and rather clumsily welded them together. That's an interesting way of going about things. The other way is to say this is how, as far as we know, the Gospel of John has been for about eighteen hundred and eighty years, so if it hasn't become a book by now, it never will become a book. So, there is an argument in favour of, not rejecting, but bracketing off that other kind of approach, taking the book as a whole, just as there is for *Hamlet*, for example. Because *Hamlet* doesn't reflect back on some actual series of events, nobody actually wants to say that 'Ur-Hamlet' is more important than *Hamlet*, which is really, in a way, I guess, a parody of what the biblical scholars tend to do. That particular difference of view has now begun to press itself on the theological profession, particularly in the United States. It's very typical, I think, that a great quarrel is in progress or was in progress a year or so ago – quarrel would be wrong, controversy – between the followers of Brevard Childs at Yale and the followers of James Barr in England, which is really a kind of classic literary confrontation on just this matter. Childs's view is that the whole canon is the formation of historical evolution, which is really the same as the historical evolution of a single book; so there is perfect justification for not breaking the canon down into its constituents and then breaking the constituents down into their constituents, but treating it as a whole, recognizing that all sorts of historical influences were brought to bear, sometimes irrelevantly, sometimes not. You see, I'm a Childsian in a way. I'm a great admirer of Barr, who takes a very strong view that the vocation of biblical scholars is to see through, as it were, the mess that history has made of the books, to what actually happened in the first place. I respect that view, but I think that Childs's view is at least equally valid.

This illustrates the point you were making earlier that one reverts to original interests without knowing it. I studied that particular controversy and the whole history of canon formation, and I found it very interesting. So that persuaded me, I think (but if I'm persuaded I better not say 'I think'), that persuaded me that there is a very important difference between what we do when we read a non-canonical book and what we do when we read a canonical one, and that this difference, though in a more shadowy way, is reflected in secular scholarship. Here is a point that I didn't make myself; it was made by John Barton. Let's take a particular book, the Book of Ecclesiastes is the one he takes. Supposing it had not got into the canon of the Jewish Bible, as it might not have done, because it could obviously be represented as an undesirable book in some ways. The Book of Revelation would be a parallel in the Christian canon. But supposing Ecclesiastes had not been included and had therefore disappeared from view, which it certainly would have done because of the rather strict Jewish tradition which kept the inside books in high profile and let the others go. Supposing instead it had been found at Qumran with certain of the other documents which had been totally lost and forgotten. Now, Barton says it wouldn't be the same book. It would be literally identical, or very close to being identical with the one that we have, but it still wouldn't be the same book because it has missed out on two thousand years of attention, and that makes all the difference, I think. It's because of this kind of problem that I got interested in hermeneutics. So, altogether I think that the Bible business – this is what started me off on this ramble – really did feed back into interests that were already present in my mind, sharpening them, I think. I'm very grateful for that long excursion into the Bible, which I now regard as completely over.

PAYNE In your Northcliffe Lectures you deal extensively with problems of canon and canonicity, a subject also that was at the centre of your Wellek Lectures. I want to ask you about the similarity – and perhaps the difference – between what you're saying now about canon in the context of history and value and what you said in *The Forms of Attention*. It seemed to me in *The Forms of Attention*, you were making the central point that what at one period in literary history might be on the circumference of attention, on the outer reaches of attention, may through various changes in value or historical processes move toward the centre; and by the same token, those things which are at the centre of attention might very well be displaced and moved to the outside. Now, that view of canon is, I would say, a gentle view. I wonder if I'm picking up correctly in your Northcliffe Lectures a slightly more confrontational edge to the issue of canon, where it's not just a matter of what is at the centre of interest, but what is at the centre of power. You speak about those institutions that make legitimate or illegitimate a particular way of dealing with texts. Am I wrong to see a difference of that sort between the earlier set of lectures and this one?

KERMODE I think all literary canons are soft canons anyway. I think they have to be simply because of the need of modernity. You see you've got to have the possibility of being modern without which literature may very well cease to interest. It could also cease to have a history, because if you're not modern you're repeating something else and its history will stop. This is a point made very beautifully by Paul de Man in one of the chapters in *Blindness and Insight*. That's the soft view, though, which is a view defined by Eliot in that sort of beautiful trick whereby he allows for a fixed, timeless canon but also allows the admission of other books to it. He argues quite rightly because they're all new, in a certain sense, and can cohabit in the canon. So that has to be the soft view. And the hard view is one that has been brought upon me by the politics of interpretation. Canons are associated with or protected by institutions, and institutions are part of a network, a hierarchy of institutions, which therefore can be represented as being a power structure, a power structure which perhaps one feels is unjust or oppressive. Then, of course, canons will be attacked by political minorities. We talk about the power of the institution. Actually we haven't got all that much power, compared with the law, for example, or even the church. We're pathetically ill-organized and without central authority in the institution of literary criticism. However, if you're in that institution, and you see it as oppressive, for reasons of race or sex or ideology or whatever, then one of the things you're going to attack, one of the things you're going to try to take over, is the canon, the visible

emblem of the decisions of the institution. In that sense,
I think it's very important to do a certain amount of
digging in and resisting, not out of enmity or disapproval
of the aspirations of feminists and blacks and so on –
certainly not; but because this move is a great deal more
destructive than the people who are making it imagine it
to be. The fact is that you can't, paradoxically, have a
canon unless you have a tradition of canon. You can't
suddenly say, let's have a new canon. That's not the way
canons work. You can't say out with Milton and in with,
I've forgotten, Zora Neale Hurston. You can't do that.
That's not the way canons are formed. That's not the way
they're broken. In fact, we don't know much about how
you break up a canon because it's hardly ever done. The
way you do it, I suppose, would be to destroy the power
of the institution that protects it. Yes, I suppose the
community of Qumran could be said to have had a canon.
They had all these different scrolls, ritual documents, so
on and so forth, mixed up with Isaiah and other books of
the Old Testament. Well, they disappeared. They were
wiped off the face of the earth, and so to all intents and
purposes were most of their books. The ones that survived
were the ones that they shared with the Orthodox Jews
and which were therefore carried on in the Jewish tradition.
The other ones were dumped in caves and they hadn't
been found until quite recently. So the way to destroy the
Qumran community's canon was to destroy the community.

PAYNE   Of course, the interesting case there is that it
wasn't because they were sectarian Jews that they were
destroyed. It was because they were Jews, isn't it?

KERMODE   That's true. They were destroyed by the
Romans, the more powerful political force.

PAYNE   You've been moving with some regularity back
and forth between two great institutions, Cambridge and
Columbia, for the past few years. Have you perceived any

fundamental differences between the way literary studies are undertaken in Cambridge and in Columbia, or, more generally, major differences in literary studies between Britain and America at this point?

KERMODE Well, it's a very large issue, and the immediate answer is yes, there are very different differences. I think the taste for the new is very much more pronounced in the United States than it is in England. That would be one way of putting it. Thus the success of literary theory over the last twenty years or so has been very much greater in America than it has here. Here, I think if you look for experiments of deconstruction, post-structuralism generally, neo-Marxism, you would look outside the major universities. You would look to the polytechnics. There are, of course, exceptions like Terry Eagleton in Oxford, Christopher Norris in Wales and so on. But on the whole, you could look at the present faculty of Cambridge, and there would be only one person in it, Stephen Heath, who in any way meets the requirement of interest in literary theory of the modern sort. This is why Heath is well known in America, and he often goes there. The rest of the people seem quite content to go on with some form of the old ways of doing things. Another difference is that – again, you see, I seem to be talking about tradition all the time – I think that the traditional way in which scholars and literary scholars are formed has been so different in the two countries. Here, the quite regular formation, in the early days of the university English curriculum, was to come from a classics department into an English department. And I think the story in the United States has been different. The whole thing is a matter of great interest because the teaching of English in America, as I understand it, and I learned this from William Riley Parker years ago, really began with the big land-grant colleges in the mid-West, which were part of the business of Americanizing immigrants. The early English departments were really speech departments, primarily, and they grew out of that. Well, the growth of English studies in England was quite different. Of course, it didn't exist at all at Oxford and Cambridge, and the first professor of English literature in England was at University College in London in 1832. Now, University College was expressly founded to meet the needs of people who couldn't go to Oxford or Cambridge. There were many reasons why you couldn't go to Oxford or Cambridge. One was that you had to be a man. Another was that you had to be a member of the Church of England. And so, two large minorities, namely women and Jews, were excluded from Oxford and Cambridge. That's why, in the lecture room where you saw me lecture the other day, you saw a Hebrew inscription around the blackboard. And Gustave Tuck was of course a Jew, and a lot of the foundation money for the institution came from Jews. English studies then were really set up for people who, through no fault of their own, could not attend Oxford and Cambridge. Having decided that these people, because of their educational disabilities, would have to study literature in English, the method of teaching English was taken over directly from the teaching of classics. English literature was then taught as if it were in a foreign language. In fact, as far as possible, they confined it to Anglo-Saxon for that reason, and to Middle English. So that is, I think, an extremely important difference between the two countries. There are many others, which go down to the level of what is taught in secondary schools, because the whole pattern of education is so different, so much more specialized in England, that the whole enterprise of teaching English starts at a different point and goes in a different direction. Anybody who tries to work in both systems, as I have done, has simply got to recognize the differences in the American system, which, since it's on the whole, I think, a very rational system, is not very difficult to do. It seems to me that the plan (whatever the performance) of undergraduate education at Columbia and dozens of other places is much more reasonable than anything that you find in England.

PAYNE   I asked you about differences in the way that English studies are carried out in both countries because when the famous MacCabe case broke at Cambridge, it was written about extensively, and as one read about it from the other side of the Atlantic, there was something in that case that seemed perhaps not so much to suggest fundamental differences between the two countries but rather – and now I'm going to ask whether this is really accurate – a sense in which that case seemed to epitomize the resistance that was going on in many English departments in America as well as in England to new movements in theory, to the influence, the impact of French and German philosophical and theoretical thinking. So, I wonder if that's so, was there something institutionally specific about that case? Is it incorrect to generalize from it?

KERMODE   I think there is something institutionally specific about it, but it is reasonable to generalize from it. The circumstances were peculiarly of Cambridge, I think, and they had to do with local rules about tenure; they had to do with the sort of animosities that traditionally spring up in certain Cambridge faculties, especially the English, which has been notable for its quarrels ever since it was founded just after the First World War. There have been some very big quarrels, notably the ones involving Leavis. The intellectual basis of Leavis's quarrel was wholly different from this one, almost totally different. I mean Leavis was opposed to literary theory, so he certainly would have been opposed to MacCabe, but that's not what they were fighting about really. The MacCabe case really did turn on an individual, and the broadening of the specific into the general was done partly by the newspapers who didn't know what they were talking about. The reporting of that business, which was not only grossly disproportionate in the attention which was paid to it but grossly inaccurate in detail, had far too much to do with what happened. Then there were things not worth considering at this level, just sort of personal bitterness against individuals which expressed itself in this way. There was lot of stupidity, I think, on both sides of the argument, and those of us who tried, because we thought we owed it to the faculty and to ourselves as senior people, to keep out of the main brawl, we, of course, were the people who really got beaten up. The whole thing, by then, had become completely irrational. And the whole question, at an institutional level, was not at all about whether post-structuralism was a good thing; it was really about whether somebody compared to somebody else was good enough to get hired again. That's really what it came down to. Naturally that involved all these other questions, the intense bitterness with which people opposed 'this French nonsense'. I'll tell you a good instance of the differences that exist between the two countries, still, that will come from an anecdote. I went to, in Cambridge, a lecture by Jacques Derrida which was to be split into two parts. It was to last for two hours, and there was to be an interval of two or three minutes to enable people who had to leave at the end of the first hour to go. It was a very interesting lecture about Kafka; in so far as Derrida's lectures are ever about something so familiar and specific, it was about Kafka. Such of my colleagues in English who went to this lecture, which was given in English, left, I think, to a man, at the interval. Now, it's inconceivable that that could happen here in London, or perhaps anywhere now in the United States. It might happen in Paris, but it wouldn't happen in any major American university. I've also heard Derrida lecture in Chicago, where the rest of us were giving our turns, and for him there had to be sort of police reinforcements. The place was so crowded, so packed, they couldn't get everybody in. So that's a difference in response to the one name really which stands out from all the others in theory. In

Cambridge, on the evening of the performance, he gave a seminar on the lecture and perhaps because he said he would take the seminar in French and not in English, even fewer people turned out, and none of my colleagues at all, not a single one. I mean my wife and I were the only people to have anything to do with English who were present at that time. Now, this again has to do with tradition. Derrida is not admired by English philosophers, whereas some American philosophers, even those in the English tradition, I think at least are willing to listen to him and talk about him, but here the attitude to Derrida is very like the attitude to Heidegger – what's he got to do with us? He doesn't belong to our kind of thinking at all. There are exceptions, of course. But there is a real opposition to this kind of speculative theoretical work, and it has to do, in some part at any rate, with that basis in the classical tradition that I mentioned earlier. Classicists usually don't concern themselves with Derrida.

PAYNE   As you look now over the current scene of literary theory – you just mentioned Derrida – what two or perhaps three theorists strike you as doing work that will endure or have major significance for the next thirty, fifty years? Who seems to you most important and influential in current thinking about literature?

KERMODE   That's a very difficult question. I'm sure, in fact, that Derrida will be of interest then. He is very much a thinker with whom one has somehow got to tune into. I'm reading an essay of his at the moment, which has not been published yet, which strikes me as absurdly long; it delays absurdly; it's not a walk through a subject, it's a dance on a subject. He's always picking up the last phrase he used and looking at it and sort of doing a little dance around it, and yet it's a deeply serious performance. I thought, and it's an obvious comparison I suppose, that the impact of Derrida will be a bit like that of Nietzsche. There will be very great arguments about what he was really talking about. There will be the people who will say, oh well, he wasn't really a philosopher at all. There will be others who will call him a philosopher above all else. There will be people who credit him or discredit him with various political arguments. I doubt whether his celebrity will be associated primarily with literary studies. I think he will be seen in the end, and perhaps is seen now, and probably would himself accept, that he belongs to the philosophical tradition. Although of course in the whole context of his thought, you are not supposed to separate philosophic texts out from other ones. Anyway, I think he is assured of a certain kind of permanence and importance.

I should have thought that Barthes, who has gone into his posthumous slump, will certainly endure simply because he writes so beautifully and because, although he says many silly things, as we all do, some of his work is of lasting importance for the study of literature. He wrote on many, many different things, of course, but I would say that Barthes was a sort of formalist, was somebody who rather brilliantly combines both descriptive technique and literary sensitivity.

I should have thought that Gerard Genette would be valuable, because it's not often in literary studies that you get something that can be built on, and I think that in his systematic study of fiction there are incompletenesses, some of which in fact he pointed out himself in a supplementary volume; but if people want to go on doing what is called narratology, then I think they will want to go on reading Genette. And they'd probably want to go on reading Todorov also, so there is, with one or two of the other French people, there is some real stuff for the future, probably, in that area.

Outside France, there is no doubt some kind of stream coming from people like Jauss and Iser which is probably not strong enough to become a predominant school but which will feed in. I think the whole, when it gets blended with Fish, you will get that kind of reader-response element in thinking about literature that is unlikely to fade away, because at its basis there's real common sense. One wonders how we got along without it, so to speak. But all these things are going to merge in a way we can't predict, aren't they? The shape of interest in literary theory and the intensity of it in twenty or twenty-five years time is strictly unpredictable. We're just guessing, where guesses are always wrong.

In America, a lot of the influence comes from outside what is technically the domain of literary studies. Hayden White, I suppose, has had an influence, coming from his work as a perfectly orthodox historian, but using a literary theory to say very interesting things about the writing of history and its rhetorical forms. The barriers in America, as in France, and to a much lesser extent here, between our subject and other subjects have been removed; or at least they've become open frontiers, and you can go back and forth across them. So historians and theologians and philosophers and literary critics are all really jostling about in very similar areas now. You get people like John Searle writing very central stuff about fiction and about the language of fiction. The linguists come in too, and the anthropologists. There is much more in the interdisciplinary work, which has its dangers. The dangers are, of course, that people get a smattering of something and apply it without really knowing it. It's very difficult to avoid that when all these disciplines have got their own structures and depths. It's like me messing about with Bible criticism. You can't really know it all. I mean, there are some books that one doesn't even trouble to read because, though they're very important, one will never really be able to understand them. The whole question, for example, of Aramaism in the New Testament is one which is closed to me. I know it's important, but how could I ever really make legitimate use of it? You've got very powerful people who do know linguistics and who move into the area of literary scholarship. Ann Banfield's book, *Unspeakable Sentences*, I thought, was impressive. So when you ask me, who are the literary theorists who are likely to have a permanent effect, it's very hard to answer because the people who might have that effect may not be in the literature field primarily. They might be historians or philosophers or anthropologists or psychoanalysts.

PAYNE Do you think there's anything to the cry of concern that has come up even from within the practice of literary theory itself that theoretical studies may be at a point of becoming extreme? I'm thinking of Todorov's now famous essay that was in *The Times Literary Supplement* about a year ago, reviewing Robert Scholes's book, *Textual Power*. Many cries of concern or of crisis in theory claim that there is a kind of antihumanism that exists within theoretical thought that perhaps endangers the life of literature itself. Is there anything to that?

KERMODE I think there is something to that. This is where I disagree with Paul de Man, whom I greatly admire and who may very well be one of the players within the field who will continue to have a powerful influence. But Paul thought that the study of literature should really be confined to very few people, that it should be very rigorous study. Well, of course, I suppose we would all agree to that, that it should be rigorous, but not that it should be confined; and few of us could match his rigour as a rhetorical analyst. The real trouble, I think, if you look at the institution as a whole in America, is that far too much of the resources of the institution are going to literary theory considered as an end in itself, almost. In fact, I read the other day in an American book that literary theory may now be regarded as the modern form of poetry. It's become the most prestigious form of literary writing. My point is that if literary study becomes entirely a matter of theory – so that undergraduates are reading *Diacritics* and even publishing articles in *Diacritics*, which really show that what you need is a certain number of assumptions and methods, not a knowledge of literature at all – then we will lose the channels by which an informed faculty communicates with students. If you lose your students, if you can't think of any way of teaching students literature as opposed to teaching them theory, then you lose literature, because nobody else now really reads what we call literature, except people who've been taught how to read it at universities. So if you stop teaching them to read it, then you might as well give up having literary theories, because you've destroyed literature – a category that some theorists want explicitly to destroy anyway. I think that is the real danger. It's necessary to keep a road open by which ordinary intelligent people can become expert to the degree that you need to be to read the best things as we judge the best things to be. Once you lose that, once your professor goes reluctantly into the undergraduate classroom to teach whatever it might be – it could be Baudelaire, Racine, anybody – once he does that reluctantly and with a sense that he's not doing real business, then I think we are in trouble. And that is what I fear, and I think the danger is much greater in this case in America than anywhere else, because of the enormous prestige attached to theory by important people in the field. I think a great many undergraduates would be totally lost given the de Man treatment of literature. He always liked to say that true reading is reading at a fearfully high level – almost destructive level – of power. You can't do that with the mass of undergraduates. At least, I don't think you can. And you've got to put things in place before you can knock them over. I gave a lecture once, one of those Trilling Seminars at Columbia, years ago now, making this point, and de Man was there, and it was the only time in my knowledge of him, which was affectionate over the years, that he was very angry with me for saying such things. He really did think that there was a sort of clerisy – or that there ought to be such a thing – which read texts with the sort of intensity that he did. But we've got to have vulgarization, I fear – *haute vulgarization*, of course.

PAYNE   You were speaking with affection and admiration about Paul de Man, which leads me to recall the first of your Northcliffe Lectures, in which you take up the question of whether literature can become a force for social or political change. One of the major criticisms that was levelled against de Man by Frank Lentricchia, and it's implied also in Eagleton's work, is that the kind of thinking about literature that de Man was advocating was antisocial, antiprogressive, designed not to promote the kind of social and political change which one might otherwise desire. Is that a legitimate concern about high theory, that it becomes detached from social action and social concerns?

KERMODE   That would be Said's line, too, of course. My guess is that de Man would have been totally untouched by that criticism. He thought of theory as a disinterested activity of the intellect, and any connections that were made with political power and so on would be up to the person making the connections. That is only a guess, of course. Now, Derrida seems to be more responsive to that kind of criticism, I think. He, more and more, seems to want to relate his intellectual activities to political issues, not to precise positions, but to a politics, anyway. That would be my guess about this, although only he can say. It's evident in any case that political texts are, like others, within his purview.

PAYNE   What I was recalling was that you said in your first lecture, as you set up the contrast between Orwell and Lewis Jones, that literature we admire seems to require a kind of detachment – a kind of superiority, I think is what you suggested – that comes out of the pastoral way of looking at the world. And that of course led you in that first lecture to challenge Eagleton and others who have taken a very different view. Is what you're saying about literature, that it requires this sense of detachment and aesthetic distance, also true of criticism? One argument made in opposition to de Man is that the social detachment of an author does not necessarily justify social detachment by the critic, who needs to enter into the public arena of debate and conversation.

KERMODE   This is a very difficult subject – it comes onto the agenda and goes off the agenda at regular intervals, doesn't it? You think of Sartre in the post-war years who was incessantly arguing for commitment. And then you think of his last critical work, if you can call it that, his psychocritical work, namely the big book about Flaubert, which doesn't seem to have any kind of very direct political applicability. So, the mood fluctuates. Then there's the question of the utility of it, anyway. Spenser was engaged in politics after all, wasn't he, but I don't think anybody's ever suggested that his engagement made very much difference. It may somewhat have reinforced the Elizabethan settlement. Swift was engaged in politics, and perhaps he's a counter-example, because it's probable that his writings did something to affect the issues, like in the case of Wood's halfpence and the *Drapier Letters*, for example. But when you think back into the great decade of political engagement for theatre, in Britain anyway, and you think of what went on at the Unity Theatre, or think of American plays like *Waiting for Lefty* and so on, what good did all that do? It hasn't affected American or British political history in any measurable way, as far as one can see. Difficulties of judgement arise over poems like Auden's 'Spain', which I, unlike many or most of his critics, think is a great political poem, but I don't expect great political poems to have an effect on what happens. I don't think Marvell's 'Horatian Ode', a truly great political poem, had any effect whatever on politics. Orwell – I suppose *Animal Farm* and *1984* have had an effect, probably an effect that he foresaw, namely that they did – the first of them coming at the end of the war when we were all in a fever about being the allies of Russia – did do something to cut down on that, to give us a real thriller-writer's terror of the totalitarian state, and in that they did have some effect. But as to criticism, again I should think of Orwell, the essay on *Boy's Weekly*, for example, which is a brilliant piece of work; but it ends with the nonsensical recommendation that there should be children's newspapers that actually talk not about public school boys but about the children of the workers. But the children of the workers wouldn't have read them. They wanted to read the other ones.

But I am myself a person of certain political convictions, but I don't think they've had much effect on what I've written. Eagleton is very well known, partly because he's the exception. But even with Raymond Williams, you don't have a feel that there's the same sort of desperate desire to get into and help to shape a working-class culture that you get in the communist writers of the thirties. It's all become very much more abstract. Williams has written a sort of treatise on Marxism and literature, as Eagleton has written a good many of them, but they always have the air, curiously enough, even more so than most recent criticism, I think, of detachment from real-life politics. They're very high-flown. Some of the things in Eagleton, as I've read him, are almost impossibly obscure. If you take very good writers who were interested, for a while, in communism, Edmund Wilson for example, you see, perhaps, how they were more naïve; but they were certainly more interested in what it meant to have a more unified or less divided society, a proletarian society. That's why I think some of Wilson's underestimated work, like *Daisy*, which is a very interesting book, is far sharper on the subject of how middle-class intellectuals should interact with workers than anything you will find in neo-Marxism. Fred Jameson is another good example, an interesting fellow, but you hardly suspect that he's ever seen a worker.

The neo-Marxist studies of Conrad with their extraordinary intellectual contortions have drifted far away from the reality of proletarian life, compared with the Marxism of the thirties. I remember talking to Julia Kristeva about this a long time ago, it must be more than fifteen years ago; we were doing a BBC radio conversation in the great days of *Tel Quel*, shortly after the '68 riots in Paris, in fact. *Tel Quel* was strongly Marxist (it's changed a lot since then), and she was actually arguing that when they'd thrashed out the theoretical problems in the pages of *Tel Quel*, they would go along to the Renault factory and explain them to the workers. I found myself saying things like, 'You must be joking. Are you serious? Is this a bluff or is this serious?' It was perfectly serious. Maybe they did it. I don't know. Maybe Terry Eagleton goes and lectures to Oxford automobile workers about Marxism, I don't know, perhaps he does.

PAYNE Is there in this hope, or perhaps illusion, that literature can make some kind of political difference, is there an attempt to answer the question, what is literature really for? Is there an overestimation of literature's value and power in some of these arguments? Or is that being too generous?

KERMODE I say some people have a vested interest in disinterest. You know the old Kantian idea that really would deprive us from having any practical effects. You remember, that was very much the mode of the New Criticism. It had its politics way, way back, of mostly a rather reactionary sort: no road through to action; the poem did not mean but be. All these things imply inactivity, except intense activity on the site of the poem. On the other hand there are those who think that that is entirely deplorable, and I'm very interested by this, which is an obsession of Paul de Man's, too. He alerts one to the sense in which impossibles are always confronting each other in intellectual fields, just as, on the question of modernity, if there were nothing but the modern, there couldn't be literature, because there would be no history of literature, and if there were no literature there couldn't be the modern. If you plant your flag on one side or other of that aporia, then you become a propagandist of one sort or another. It seems to me that the situation is very much the same concerning the practical impact of literature. Some believe that the value of literature arises from its disinterest; if you believe that, then the question of its practical effect is totally unimportant. On the other hand, some believe that that is a myth and that the only measure of value would be a quite different one, namely that of practical effect, but also the involvement of a large generality of people in the effect. That's why there's this uneasy feeling about popular literature, which we have in our community at the moment. It's something that Eagleton is unhappy about; he, like so many other people, has a sense that the high–low distinction in literature is a false one, so that we get people with bad consciences about high literature taking on Bob Dylan, for example, or taking on other matters that are far less obviously impressive than Bob Dylan. So you get these divisions, which are inherent in the subject, I think.

That's the real trouble. It's not, I think, that people divide naturally into the disinterested and the practical; it is that literature divides that way. All this is partly caused by our erecting, as is very often said nowadays, a whole category called 'literature', which we, after all, didn't really have until quite recently. The word was there, but the idea that there were certain books which were literature and certain books which were not was not formulated. It was a necessary formulation, given the social context in which we developed literature. In fact, in a sense, it's always been around in essence, because the Greeks knew the difference between Homer and Homer's imitators. Either you were like Plato and thought that Homer was a danger to the state or you thought that he was the cement of the state, because he was very central to its religion. Either you took one view or you took the other. They didn't say Homer is literature and whosit is not literature, but there was something like that on their minds. They attended to Homer with a special kind of attention, more attention and a different quality of attention than they gave to other people, and that is what, after all, we mean when we say that Shakespeare is literature and that Deloney, say, is marginally so, popular literature. We certainly have to make these distinctions, because without them the whole thing becomes totally unmanageable. If literature is not a separate category, what the hell are we going to do in English departments? Pick up anything and read it? It really is a practical issue. There has to be a category of literature.

PAYNE I'm curious here about what may have been the impact on your own thinking of your work on the Modern Masters series. I may have this chronologically wrong – we haven't talked personally about this before – but just from reading your books it seems that about the time you were beginning to edit that series, the extent of your references in your critical writing to people we might think of as non-literary figures begins to be much more extensive. Was there an influence on your work as a critic that came from your work on the Modern Masters series, in which you were dealing with, admittedly, introductory texts, but many of them of very high power?

KERMODE I don't know. One can never really be sure about such questions, but I think the history was a bit like this. I'd been in America for the academic year 1969–70. It was the time of the Cambodian invasion, in the spring of 1970. I was at Wesleyan in Connecticut, and I was very impressed by the way in which the students seemed to be interested in almost everything except literature. They were very keen on Norman Brown who had taught at Wesleyan until recently, and Marcuse, and others; and it struck me that this really was the age of the guru. Chomsky, of course, was a very big name at the time too. When I got back to England, I was asked to lunch by Mark Collins, the publisher, and he asked me to edit a huge, full-scale, multi-volume history of English literature. I said, don't do it, I think it's absolutely crazy, wrong time, and so on. The point I was making was that it may not be possible, and in any case if it is possible we don't know how to do it. He said, well, what would you like to do, and the Modern Masters series was born at that moment. It was signed up the next day. In a way, what I took on was a guru series; it wasn't a planned thing at all. It just happened that way. It was all done in a great rush, and it was a great success. It seemed my hunch was right, and it provided a form of popular literature. These books were so very cheap; they sold; some of them were as cheap as 25 pence in those days, and the big fat ones, like the Freud, which we considered a double volume, was only about 45 pence. So they sold like hotcakes. Later on, of course, this feeling diminished. The book on Chomsky had a most fabulous success in about twenty languages, and altogether it must have sold over half a million copies. But it was a little book and a serious book; there was nothing about Chomsky's politics, or hardly anything, in it, and very little technical linguistics. When Lyons, the author, saw that it was being used as a textbook, he felt that it ought to have some more meat in it, so there was a second edition which had a lot more linguistics in it. People wanted to know about these people rather than to know in detail what they said. Some of them were very serious, of course, the Wittgenstein, Freud, Popper and so on.

The guru age really ended somewhere around about 1980. The books that we've produced in that series since, like the Adorno or the Saussure, have been really much more subject-oriented than the early ones were. It's good that that particular sort of hero worship has died down. I think it crops up again, particularly in the States with people like Derrida and to some extent Bloom. Names are still magic in some sense, but not the way they were then.

To come back to your question, I think I was so busy editing these things, I don't really think much adhered, you know. There was a book on Fanon. I couldn't tell you anything about Fanon now; I think he's completely out of my head. I suppose I must have learned something from doing all that, but I can't remember what it was now. It may have made a difference, but on the whole I think probably rather little. After all, during the seventies my own main reading was in the Bible, which none of those books had anything to do with.

PAYNE We were speaking of Isaiah Berlin briefly before we started this interview. He makes that wonderful distinction between the hedgehog and the fox, based on the famous Greek fragment. From reading your books, there's rather more of the impression of an intellectual fox than of a hedgehog, of someone who, if I may say so, seems very open and receptive to a wide range of intellectual subjects and intellectual styles, who has a desire to move rather freely not only through the literary tradition but also from it over into others, despite what you say about the necessity of keeping the literary shop open. So, at a time when there seem to be so many system-builders, your work rather seems a bit more sceptical of system and of structured theory. Is that right?

KERMODE I think that's true. I think I am, if it's possible to be naïvely sceptical, I think that's probably what I am. Of the hedgehog and the fox narrative, if you had to choose, I think you've chosen right. It probably would require a third animal, I think, perhaps a hybrid.

PAYNE A foxy hedgehog.

KERMODE It is a famous and, in a way, a just distinction, I think. But I can't remember who he gives as instances of the two, now, can you remember?

PAYNE   Plato is on the hedgehog side. I seem to remember the ones on the hedgehog side rather than on the other side. But Berlin's book is about Tolstoy finally, and I think the point is that Tolstoy was, in a sense, both, not even just at different times in his career, but, in fact, within the same mind at once. I suppose I was taking a risk matching that characterization with your thinking, because the one critic who seems to have, in some remarkable ways, written very differently but on almost exactly the same subjects that you have is, of course, Frye, even to the extent of doing an edition of *The Tempest* and writing now on the Bible.

KERMODE   Oh, Frye is a hedgehog.

PAYNE   Oh, absolutely a hedgehog, and I think that's one of the very curious but very interesting things about taking up any of these subjects now and finding both of you writing about a whole succession of them, even including some of the same authors, such as Spenser and Milton and Eliot and Stevens. The method of the approach, the intellectual style is so different, even despite Frye's disclaimer that all his structure is to be dismantled the very next time you pick up the next book and read it.

KERMODE   I greatly admire *Anatomy of Criticism*, which probably had more effect on me than any other modern book of criticism. I knew about the Blake book; I say that because I can't remember at that time whether I had read it. I read *Anatomy of Criticism* when it came out. Frye didn't mean a great deal to me as a name, right then, but I saw, and said in a review, that this is certainly a great book, in a sense; it's a book that's going to survive its arguments. It's written beautifully. He's the best writer of critical prose we have. There are two things I would say about him. One is that his kind of mind is quite different from mine. He's got a very much greater synthetic power than I have. He also commands, and really commands, vast arrays of material which I don't. The thing I have against him is precisely that there's only one way he does things. There were some books in the early sixties, including a couple on Shakespeare, that were still exciting, but were still being moved by the force that moved the *Anatomy*. Then he began to see that the conjuror had actually demonstrated all his tricks in the earlier book and that you were just seeing slight variations on them. I reviewed a book of his in the *New York Review* about Shakespeare's tragedies, where he had invented a kind of epicycle to the system to do the tragedies. I said that all Frye's systems and cycles are really just like a memory theory, they're a mnemonic device that enables him to get around literature very easily. And he wrote me a rather sour letter saying that I thought you would have realized that long ago. Just like Frances Yates.

PAYNE What was the nature of your association with Frances Yates and with the Warburg Institute?

KERMODE I knew Frances for the last thirty years of her life, more or less, and admired her very much. She's the kind of scholar that I think we could actually do with more of, although her practice was certainly a dangerous one. She was, of course, enormously learned and always ready to acquire new information. She was beautifully equipped linguistically in all sorts of ways; but when she'd gather the information, she always had a theory about it. That's fine, provided you're willing to get off the horse when the road runs out. But she would gallop across the country, anyhow. The book on the Elizabethan theatre, for example, really depends on a very complicated assumption that Burbage's workmen would have read Dee's Euclid. And there were other weak links like that. She wrote wonderfully exciting books like *The Valois Tapestries*, which has always been one of my favourite books, but which, again, I dare say, has got very weak links in it somewhere. But I liked her, putting it weakly. I thought she was a marvellous woman, partly because she brought into very recondite scholarship this terrific spirit of adventure which you don't often get. Her book on the French academies, which the experts say is probably her best book, contains thousands of days of hard labour, and yet it has all the adventurousness of something that's never been done before, something which changes our whole view about certain educational practices in the Renaissance. To do this endless labour and yet still be spirited, and to fly off, as she did towards the end of her life, with all these theories about the last plays of Shakespeare and all that stuff about Rosicrucianism – well, there was something in it obviously – but there was a wildness in it, too. Yes, if I had to choose between being a Frances Yates kind of scholar and a Northrop Frye kind, I would certainly want to be the Frances Yates kind, but I'm incapable of being either, so the question doesn't arise.

PAYNE   There is at least one thing in common about the two of them, I think, and that is that neither of them had a traditional kind of education. Frances took, I believe, an external degree from the University of London, and then a marginal professional appointment quite late in her career. Frye says somewhere that not having to go through the rigours of getting a Ph.D left him free to read Spengler and Indian epics and other such things.

KERMODE   I do think that Ph.Ds can be a perfect nuisance, because they do take up good reading years, sometimes on too strict a topic. Frances had, obviously, a better education than most of us. She had good Greek, Latin, Italian, French, German. How many scholars could you say that of quickly? And if she needed another language, she went and learned it. She was very quick at picking up languages.

PAYNE   But largely self-taught?

KERMODE   Largely self-taught, I think, yes. And then she homed in on the Warburg when it arrived in London; it was obviously her scene. And she had some independent means, so was not quite in the position that some others have been in of having to have a job. You see, it's important not to have to, even though it's rather tough not to. And then, of course, she was unpaid for years at the Warburg before she finally became a reader or something. But you couldn't hope for a better education, I think, than to work with people like Saxl and Gombrich, all those people around there. It was an education to work with them. So I don't feel sorry for her in that respect, and she was always an enormously hard worker. She had the best part of half a century of solid output, which was quite something. And some of those things are just irreplaceable, aren't they? That essay on Queen Elizabeth as Astraea can never be replaced, and it's absolutely changed the whole view of the subject. Anybody who wants to know about the iconography of Elizabeth has got to read Yates's essay, no question. That's why I understand why people choose scholarship. It shouldn't be chosen on the assumption that it doesn't take imagination, though; that's the mistake people make.

PAYNE   What are your own plans for writing at this point?

KERMODE   Because I edit the Oxford Authors, I've got to edit an Oxford Author. I'm going to be editing Marvell, which I've done before actually, so that's not going to be a tremendous load. And that will see me through to the end of this year, anyway, easily. Then, there are other projects; one of them I'm not supposed to talk about, so I won't. I haven't, at the moment, got a plan to write another book. I'll have to wait for someone to ask me to give four or six lectures; that's the way to do it. There are many other things that I'd vaguely like to do.

Frank Kermode: *A Bibliography, 1947–1988*

Compiled by Keith Walker

1947

1 'A note on the History of Massinger's "The Fatal Dowry" in the Eighteenth Century', *Notes and Queries*, vol. 192, pp. 186–7.
2 'The Art of Theodore Powys, Ironist', *Welsh Review*, vol. 6, no. 3, pp. 205–19.

1948

3 'The Theme of Auden's Poetry', *Rivista di letterature moderne*, vol. 3, pp. 1–14.
4 'What is Shakespeare's Henry VIII about?', *Durham University Journal*, n.s., vol. 9, pp. 48–55. Reprinted in Waith, E. M. (ed.), *Shakespeare: The Histories* (Englewood Cliffs, NJ: Prentice-Hall, 1965) pp. 168–79; and in Armstrong, W. A. (ed.), *Shakespeare's Histories* (Harmondsworth, Middx: Penguin, 1972) pp. 256–69.

1949

5 'The Date of Cowley's *Davidies*', *Review of English Studies*, vol. 25, pp. 154–8.
6 Review of *Les Chansons Elizabéthaines* by F. Delattre and C.

Chemin (1948), *Review of English Studies*, vol. 25, pp. 356–7.

7 Review of *Music and Poetry of the English Renaissance* by Bruce Pattison (1948), *Review of English Studies*, vol. 25, pp. 265–9.

1950

8 'The Private Imagery of Henry Vaughan', *Review of English Studies*, n.s. vol. 1, pp. 206–25.

9 'Richardson and Fielding', *Cambridge Journal*, vol. 4, pp. 106–14. Reprinted in Spector, R. D. (ed.), *Essays on the Eighteenth Century Novel* (Bloomington, Ind.: Indiana University Press, 1964); and in Iser, W. (ed.), *Henry Fielding und der englische Roman des 18. Jahrhunderts* (Darmstadt, 1972).

10 'Yahoos and Houynhnms', *Notes and Queries*, vol. 195, pp. 317–18.

1952

11 (Ed.), *English Pastoral Poetry from the Beginnings to Marvell* (London: Harrap; New York: Barnes and Noble; New York: Norton, 1972).

12 'The Argument of Marvell's "Garden" ', *Essays in Criticism*, vol. 2, pp. 225–41. Reprinted in Keast, W. R. (ed.), *Seventeenth Century English Poetry* (New York: Oxford University Press, 1962); in Carey, John (ed.), *Andrew Marvell* (Harmondsworth, Middx.: Penguin, 1969); and in Calhoun, T. O. and Potter, J. M. (eds), *Andrew Marvell: 'The Garden'* (Columbus, Ohio: Ohio State University Press, 1970).

13 'A Spenser Crux: "The Faerie Queene", II.v.12.7–9', *Notes and Queries*, vol. 197, p. 161.

14 'Two Notes on Marvell', *Notes and Queries*, vol. 197, pp. 317–30.

1953

15 'Milton's Hero', *Review of English Studies*, vol. 4, pp. 317–30.
16 ' "Samson Agonistes" and Hebrew Prosody', *Durham University Journal*, vol. 14, pp. 59–63.

1954

17 (Ed.), *The Tempest* (London: Methuen) xxxviii, 167 pp. The Arden Shakespeare, 'Fifth Edition' (i.e. of Morton Luce's old Arden edition). 'Sixth' (second) edition: 1958 (Cambridge, Mass.: Harvard University Press).
18 'Donne Allusions in Howell's Familiar Letters', *Notes and Queries*, n.s. vol. 1, p. 337.

1955

19 'Opinion, Truth, and Value', *Essays in Criticism*, vol. 5, pp. 181–7. (See Winifred Nowottny, *Essays in Criticism*, vol. 4 (1954) pp. 282ff).

1956

20 Cutts, J. P. and Kermode, Frank (eds), *Seventeenth Century Songs now First Printed from a Bodleian Manuscript* (Reading: University Department of Fine Art) 37pp.
21 'Definitions of Love', *Review of English Studies*, vol. 7, pp. 183–5.
22 'A Myth of Catastrophe', *Listener*, 8 November, pp. 745–6; 15 November, pp. 791–2.
23 'Persevering with the "Metaphysicals" ', *Essays in Criticism*, vol. 6, pp. 205–14.
24 'The Rest of T. E. Hulme', *Essays in Criticism*, vol. 6, pp. 460–5.

1957

25 *John Donne* (London: Longmans for the British Council) 48pp.; Rev. edn, 1961, Writers and Their Work Series. Reprinted in *British Writers and Their Work*, no. 4 (Lincoln, Nebr.: University of Nebraska Press, 1964); and in *Shakespeare, Spenser, Donne* (1971).

26 *Romantic Image* (London: Routledge) xii, 171pp. (New York: Chilmark, 1963; New York: Vintage Books, 1964; London: Collins/Fontana, 1971) pp. 1–29 reprinted in Polleta, G. T. (ed.), *Issues in Contemporary Literary Criticism* (Boston, Mass.: Little, Brown, 1973).

27 'American Miltonists and English Reviewers', *Essays in Criticism*, vol. 7, pp. 196–207.

28 'A Crux in "The Tempest" III.i.15', *The Times Literary Supplement*, 29 November, p. 728.

29 'Dissociation of Sensibility', *Kenyon Review*, vol. 19, pp. 169–94. Reprinted in *Romantic Image* (1957) and in Hollander, John (ed.), *Modern Poetry* (New York: Oxford University Press, 1968), pp. 318–39.

30 'Dryden: A Poet's Poet', *Listener*, 30 May, pp. 877–8.

31 Letter to the editor, *Twentieth Century*, vol. 162, pp. 582–5. A reply to Donald Davie's review of *Romantic Image*, *Twentieth Century*, vol. 162, pp. 458–68.

1958

32 'Adam's Curse', *Encounter*, vol. 10, no. 6 (June) pp. 76–8 (Yeats).

33 'Coral Islands', *Spectator*, 22 August, p. 257 (Golding). Reprinted in *Puzzles and Epiphanies* (1962).

34 'Eliot on Poetry', *International Literary Annual*, vol. 1, pp. 131–4.

35 'Fit Audience', *Spectator*, 30 May, pp. 705–6 (Salinger). Reprinted in *Puzzles and Epiphanies* (1962).

36 'The Gaiety of Language', *Spectator*, 3 October, p. 454 (Stevens).

37 ' "A Mode of Thinking Congenial to his Nature" ', *Essays*

in Criticism, vol. 8, pp. 298–303. (Review of *Shakespeare and his Comedies* by J. R. Brown).
38 'Mr E. M. Forster as a Symbolist', *Listener*, 2 January, pp. 17–18. Reprinted in *Puzzles and Epiphanies* (1962) as 'The One Orderly Product'.
39 'Mr Wilson's People', *Spectator*, 21 November, pp. 705–6. Reprinted in *Puzzles and Epiphanies* (1962).
40 'The New Novelists: An Enquiry', *London Magazine*, vol. 5, no. 11 (November) pp. 21–5 (part of a symposium). Reprinted in *Puzzles and Epiphanies* (1962) as 'Durrell and Others'.
41 'Pasternak's Novel', *Spectator*, 5 September, p. 315.
42 'Rigour and Abundance', *Spectator*, 12 December, p. 864 (Keats).

1959

43 'Homage to Pleasure', *Spectator*, 10 July, p. 41 (Wordsworth).
44 'The Myth-Kitty', *Spectator*, 11 September, p. 339 (Coleridge). Reprinted in *Puzzles and Epiphanies* (1962).
45 'On David Jones', *Encounter*, vol. 13, no. 5 (November) pp. 76–9. Reprinted in *Puzzles and Epiphanies* (1962).
46 'Pasternak's Life', *Spectator*, 8 May, p. 667. Reprinted in *Puzzles and Epiphanies* (1962).
47 'Puzzles and Epiphanies', *Spectator*, 13 November, pp. 675–6 (Joyce). Reprinted in *Puzzles and Epiphanies* (1962).
48 Review of *Anatomy of Criticism* by Northrop Frye, *Review of English Studies*, vol. 10, pp. 317–23. Reprinted in *Puzzles and Epiphanies* (1962).
49 'Second Nature', *Spectator*, 2 January, pp. 19–20 (Valéry). Reprinted in *Puzzles and Epiphanies* (1962).
50 'What becomes of Sweeney?', *Spectator*, 10 April, p. 513 (T. S. Eliot).

1960

51 (Ed.), *The Living Milton: Essays by Various Hands* (London: Routledge) x, 180pp.; reissued 1962, 1963 (New York: Macmillan).

52 *Wallace Stevens* (Edinburgh: Oliver and Boyd) viii, 134pp. (New York: Grove Press, Writers and Critics Series, 1961). Pp. 24–48 reprinted in Ehrenpreis, Irvin (ed.),*Wallace Stevens* (Englewood Cliffs, NJ: Prentice-Hall, 1972).

53 'Adam Unparadised', in Kermode, Frank (ed.), *The Living Milton* (1960) pp. 85–123. Reprinted in *Shakespeare, Spenser, Donne* (1971) and in Dyson, A. E. and Lovelock, J. (eds), *Milton: 'Paradise Lost': A Casebook* (London: Macmillan, 1973).

54 'Beckett, Snow and Pure Poetry', *Encounter*, vol. 15, no. 1 (July) pp. 73–7. Reprinted in *Puzzles and Epiphanies* (1962).

55 'The Cave of Mammon', in Brown, J. R. and Harris, B. (eds), *Elizabethan Poetry* (London: Edward Arnold) pp. 151–73. Reprinted in *Shakespeare, Spenser, Donne* (1971).

56 'Counter-Revolution', *Spectator*, 1 July, pp. 25–6 (G. Hough). Reprinted in *Puzzles and Epiphanies* (1962).

57 'Fourth Dimension', *Review of English Literature*, vol. 1, no. 2, pp. 73–7 (Durrell). Reprinted in *Puzzles and Epiphanies* (1962).

58 'Hunter and Shaman', *Spectator*, 1 April, pp. 477–8 (the 1890s). Reprinted in *Puzzles and Epiphanies* (1962).

59 'The Interpretation of the Times', *Encounter*, vol. 15, no. 3 (September) pp. 71–6 (Isherwood). Reprinted in *Puzzles and Epiphanies* (1962).

60 'Mr Waugh's Cities', *Encounter*, vol. 15, no. 5 (November) pp. 63–70. Reprinted in *Puzzles and Epiphanies* (1962).

61 'Old Orders Changing', *Encounter*, vol. 15, no. 2 (August) pp. 72–6 (Allen Tate and Giuseppe di Lampedusa). Reprinted in *Puzzles and Epiphanies* (1962); part reprinted in Squires, J. R. (ed.), *Allen Tate and his Work* (Minneapolis: University of Minnesota Press, 1972 (pp. 140–8; part translated into Italian as Preface to *I Padri* (1964).

62 'A Short View of Musil', *Encounter*, vol. 15, no. 6 (December) pp. 64–75. Reprinted in *Puzzles and Epiphanies* (1962).

63 'Sillies', *Spectator*, 9 September, pp. 377–8 (Bloomsbury). Reprinted in *Puzzles and Epiphanies* (1962).

64 'The Words of the World', *Encounter*, vol. 14, no. 4 (April) pp. 45–50 (Stevens).

1961

65 'The Banquet of Sense', *Bulletin of the John Rylands Library*, vol. 44, pp. 68–99. Reprinted in *Shakespeare, Spenser, Donne* (1971).

66 'Definitions of Culture', *New Statesman*, 2 June, pp. 880–2 (R. Wollheim).

67 'Edmund Wilson and Mario Praz', *Encounter*, vol. 16, no. 5 (May) pp. 69–73. Reprinted in *Puzzles and Epiphanies* (1962).

68 'The European View of Christopher Brennan', *Australian Letters*, vol. 3, pp. 57–63.

69 'Henry Miller and John Betjeman', *Encounter*, vol. 16, no. 3 (March) pp. 69–75. Reprinted in *Puzzles and Epiphanies* (1962).

70 'Interesting but Tough', *Spectator*, 3 March, pp. 298–9 (Donne).

71 'The Mature Comedies', in Brown, J. R. and Harris, B. (eds), *Early Shakespeare* (London: Edward Arnold) pp. 211–27.

72 'Mr Greene's Eggs and Crosses', *Encounter*, vol. 16, no. 4 (April), pp. 69–75. Reprinted in *Puzzles and Epiphanies* (1962).

73 'Notes Toward a Supreme Fiction: A Commentary', *Annali dell' Instituto Universitario Orientale, Sezione Germanica* (Naples), vol. 4, pp. 173–201.

74 'The Novels of William Golding', *International Literary Annual*, vol. 3, pp. 11–29. Reprinted in *Puzzles and Epiphanies* (1962).

75 'Poet and Dancer before Diaghilev', *Partisan Review*, vol. 28, pp. 48–75. An abridged version of the essay in *Puzzles and Epiphanies* (1962).

76 'Some Recent Studies in Shakespeare and Jacobean Drama', *Studies in English Literature*, vol. 1, pp. 119–28.

77 'The Spider and the Bee', *Spectator*, 31 March, pp. 448–9 (Yeats).

1962

78 (Ed. with an introduction), *Discussions of John Donne* (Boston: D. C. Heath) xii, 160pp.
79 *Puzzles and Epiphanies: Essays and Reviews 1958–61* (London: Routledge; New York: Chilmark, xii, 234pp). Reprints items 33, 35, 38, 39, 40, 41, 44, 45, 46, 47, 49, 54, 56, 57, 58, 59, 60, 61, 62, 63, 67, 69, 72, 74, 75.
80 'Allusions to Omar', *New Statesman*, 3 August, pp. 146–7 (FitzGerald). Reprinted in *Continuities* (1968).
81 'Bernard Malamud', *New Statesman*, 30 March, pp. 452–3. Reprinted in *Continuities* (1968).
82 'Jonathan the First', *New Statesman*, 14 September, pp. 321–2 (Swift).
83 'Lawrence in his Letters', *New Statesman*, 23 March, pp. 422–3.
84 'Loie Fuller', *Theatre Arts*, vol. 46 (September) pp. 8–12.
85 'Myth, Reality and Fiction', *Listener*, 30 August, pp. 311–13. (Iris Murdoch, Graham Green, A. Wilson, Ivy Compton-Burnett, C. P. Snow, J. Wain, Muriel Spark).
86 'One Hand Clapping', *New Statesman*, 8 June , pp. 831–2 (Salinger). Reprinted in *Continuities* (1968).
87 'Pascal for Unbelievers', *New Statesman*, 4 May, pp. 637–8.
88 'Waiting for Godeau', *New Statesman*, 2 November, pp. 622–3. Reprinted in *Continuities* (1968).
89 'Zemblances', *New Statesman*, 9 November, pp. 671–2 (Nabokov). Reprinted in *Continuities* (1968).

1963

90 *William Shakespeare: The Final Plays: 'Pericles', 'Cymbeline', 'The Winter's Tale', 'The Tempest', 'The Two Noble Kinsmen'* (London: Longmans for the British Council) 59pp., Writers and Their Work Series. Reprinted in Dobrée, Bonamy (ed.), *Shakespeare: The Writer and his Work* (London: Longmans, 1964); and in *Shakespeare, Spenser, Donne* (1971).
91 (Ed.), *William Shakespeare: The Winter's Tale* (New York:

The New American Library) 223pp. The Signet Classic Shakespeare.

92 'Afterword', *Tom Jones* by Henry Fielding (New York: The New American Library), pp. 855–62.

93 'Amateur of Grief', *New Statesman*, 7 June, pp. 865–6 (Dowson). Reprinted in *Continuities* (1968).

94 'Between Two Galazies', *Encounter*, vol. 20, no. 2 (February) pp. 76–82. (McLuhan). Reprinted in Stearn, Gerald Emanuel (ed.), *McLuhan Hot and Cool* (Harmondsworth, Middx.: Penguin, 1968) pp. 173–80.

95 'Colette', *New York Review of Books*, 28 January, pp. 15–16 (J. B. Priestley).

96 'Edifying Symbols', *New Statesman*, 12 July, pp. 45–6 (C. C. O'Brien). Reprinted in *Continuities* (1968).

97 'The Glass Menagerie', *New Statesman*, 15 March, p. 388 (Salinger). Reprinted in *Continuities* (1968).

98 'The House of Fiction: Interviews with Seven English Novelists', *Partisan Review*, vol. 30, pp. 61–82 (Ivy Compton-Burnett, Graham Greene, Iris Murdoch, C. P. Snow, Muriel Spark, J. Wain, A. Wilson).

99 'Jonah', *New Statesman*, 12 April, p. 521 (Henry Miller). Reprinted in *Continuities* (1968).

100 'Novels of the Thaw', *New Statesman*, 22 March, pp. 424–5 (Russian novels).

101 'The Prime of Miss Muriel Spark', *New Statesman*, 27 September, pp. 397–8. Reprinted in *Continuities* (1968).

102 'Reading Eliot Today', *Nation*, vol. 197 (26 October) pp. 263–4.

103 'Spenser and the Allegorists', *Proceedings of the British Academy 1962*, vol. 48, pp. 261–97. The British Academy Warton Lecture for 1962. Reprinted in Alpers, Paul (ed.), *Edmund Spenser* (Harmondsworth, Middx.: Penguin, 1969); and in *Shakespeare, Spenser, Donne* (1971).

1964

104 *The Patience of Shakespeare* (Toronto: Longmans) iv, 19pp. A lecture delivered at Columbia University on 23 April 1964. Reprinted in *Encounter*, vol. 23, no. 5 (November)

pp. 3–10; and in *Shakespeare, Spenser, Donne* (1971).

105 'Afterword', *Middlemarch* by George Eliot (New York: The New American Library) pp. 813–23.

106 'Beckett Country', *New York Review of Books*, 19 March, pp. 9–11. Reprinted in *Continuities* (1968).

107 'The Case for William Golding', *New York Review of Books*, 30 April, pp. 3–4. Reprinted in *Continuities* (1968).

108 'Contemplation and Method', *Sewanee Review*, vol. 72, pp. 124–31 (A. Tate). Reprinted in *Continuities* (1968).

109 '*The Faerie Queene*, I and V', *Bulletin of the John Rylands Library*, vol. 47, pp. 123–50. Reprinted in *Shakespeare, Spenser, Donne* (1971).

110 'Hemingway's Last Novel', *New York Review of Books*, 11 June, pp. 4–6. Reprinted in *Continuities* (1968).

111 'Isadora', *New York Review of Books*, 5 March, p. 7 (Isadora Duncan).

112 'Lear at Lincoln Center', *New York Review of Books*, 25 June, pp. 4–5 (Peter Brook).

113 'The Man in the Closet', *New York Review of Books*, 3 December, pp. 33–6 (Eric Bentley).

114 'Mozart and the Enlightenment', *New Statesman*, 24 April, pp. 644–6.

115 'Players and Painted Stage', in Donoghue, Denis (ed.), *The Integrity of Yeats* (Cork: Mercier) pp. 47–57.

116 'The Shakespearian Rag', *New York Review of Books*, 24 September, pp. 9–10 (Jan Kott).

117 'That Time, This Time', *New Statesman*, 16 October, pp. 578–9 (myth). Reprinted in *Continuities* (1968).

118 'Tradition and the New Art: Interviews with Harold Rosenberg and Ernst Gombrich', *Partisan Review*, vol. 31, pp. 241–52.

119 'TV Dinner', *New York Review of Books*, 20 August, pp. 15–16 (McLuhan).

120 'What is Art?', *New York Review of Books*, 20 February, pp. 1–2 (Gombrich).

121 'Yonder Shakespeare, Who is He?' *New York Review of Books*, 9 January, pp. 1–3.

1965

122 (Ed.), *Four Centuries of Shakespearian Criticism* (New York: Avon Books), 571pp.

123 *On Shakespeare's Learning* (Middletown, Conn.: Center for Advanced Studies, Wesleyan University) 25pp. Reprinted in *Bulletin of the John Rylands Library*, vol. 48, pp. 207–26; and in *Shakespeare, Spenser, Donne* (1971). A shorter version appears in *Wesleyan University Center for Advanced Studies: Monday Evening Press*, vol. 2, pp. 7–10.

124 (Ed.), *Spenser: Selections from the Minor Poems and 'The Faerie Queene'* (London: Oxford University Press) 233pp.

125 'All Mod Cons', *New Statesman*, 16 July, pp. 85–6 (the modern). Reprinted in *Continuities* (1968).

126 'Deep Frye', *New York Review of Books*, 22 April, pp. 10–12. Reprinted in *Continuities* (1968).

127 'Eliot's Dream', *New Statesman*, 19 February, pp. 280–1.

128 'A Hero in Bad Faith: Sartre and the Anti-Novel', *New Statesman*, 24 September, pp. 439–40. Reprinted in *Continuities* (1968).

129 'Herzog', *New Statesman*, 5 February, pp. 200–1. Reprinted in *Continuities* (1968).

130 'Life and Death of the Novel', *New York Review of Books*, 28 October, pp. 5–6 (Fielding, Smollett, Jane Austen).

131 'Modern Poetry and Tradition', *Yearbook of Comparative and General Literature*, vol. 14, pp. 5–15.

132 'New and Non-New', *Partisan Review*, vol. 32, pp. 272–6 (H.Rosenberg).

133 'The Novel as Jerusalem: Muriel Spark's *Mandelbaum Gate*', *Atlantic Monthly*, vol. 216 (October) pp. 92–8. Reprinted in *Continuities* (1968).

134 'The Old Amalaki', *New York Review of Books*, 17 June, pp. 18–20 (Isherwood). Reprinted in *Continuities* (1968).

135 Preface, *Trial by Battle* by David Piper, rev. edn (New York: Chilmark; London: Collins, 1966) pp. 5–8.

136 'Rammel', *New Statesman*, 14 May, pp. 765–6 (Alan Sillitoe). Reprinted in *Continuities* (1968).

137 'Time of Your Life', *New York Review of Books*, 28 January, pp. 15–16 (J. B. Priestley).

138 'Whom the Gods Loathe', *Encounter*, vol. 24, no. 3 (March) pp. 74–5 (Max Beerbohm).

1966

139 'A Babylonish Dialect', *Sewanee Review* ('T. S. Eliot Special Issue'), vol. 74, pp. 225–37. Reprinted in Tate, Allen (ed.), *T. S. Eliot: The Man and his Work* (London: Chatto and Windus, 1967); and in *Continuities* (1968).

140 'The Calendar of Modern Letters', *New Statesman*, 2 September, p. 320.

141 'Dante', *New Statesman*, 7 January, pp. 15–16. Reprinted in *Continuities* (1968).

142 'Edmund Wilson's Achievement', *Encounter*, vol. 26, no. 5 (May) pp. 61–70. Reprinted in *Continuities* (1968).

143 'The Enduring Lear', *New York Review of Books*, 12 May, pp. 12–14.

144 'The Future of an Elite', *Encounter*, vol. 27, no. 1 (July) pp. 23–7 (the Franks Report on Oxford).

145 'Marvell Transprosed', *Encounter*, vol. 27, no. 5 (November) pp. 77–84.

146 'Modernisms: Cyril Connolly and Others', *Encounter*, vol. 26, no. 3 (March) pp. 53–8. Reprinted in *Continuities* (1968) and in Bergonzi, Bernard (ed.), *Innovations* (London: Macmillan, 1968) pp. 66–92.

147 'Modernisms Again: Objects, Jokes and Art', *Encounter*, vol. 26, no. 4 (April) pp. 65–74. Reprinted in *Continuities* (1968) and in Lodge, David (ed.) *20th Century Literary Criticism* (London: Longmans, 1972).

148 'The New Apocalyptists', *Partisan Review*, vol. 33, pp. 339–61.

149 Preface, *Five Women* by Robert Musil, trans. Eithne Wilkins and Ernst Kaiser (New York: Chilmark). Reprinted in *Modern Essays* (1971).

150 Preface, *The Poet Speaks: Interviews with Contemporary Poets*, ed. Peter Orr (London: Routledge; New York: Barnes and Noble) pp. ix–xii.

151 'Robert Musil', *Kenyon Review*, vol. 28, pp. 224–30.

152 'Some Stevens Letters', *Encounter*, vol. 27, no. 4 (October)

pp. 25–37. Reprinted in *Continuities* (1968).

153 'Tragedy and Revolution', *Encounter*, vol. 27, no. 2 (August) pp. 83–5 (Raymond Williams).

154 'The University and the Literary Public', in Stroup, T. B. (ed.), *The Humanities and the Understanding of Reality* (Lexington, KY: Kentucky University Press) pp. 55–74.

155 'The Viennese Muses', *New York Review of Books*, 15 December, pp. 16–20 (Mozart).

156 (Ed.), *Andrew Marvell: Selected Poetry* (New York: The New American Library) xlviii, 189pp., The Signet Classics Poetry Series. pp. vii-xxx Reprinted in *The Metaphysical Poets* (1969).

157 *The Sense of an Ending: Studies in the Theory of Fiction* (New York: Oxford University Press) xii, 187pp. The Mary Flexner Lectures delivered at Bryn Mawr College in 1965. Pp. 127–52 reprinted in Burns, E. and T. (eds), *Sociology of Literature and Drama* (1973).

158 'Forecasts from Hippo', *Listener*, 31 August, pp. 278–9 (St Augustine).

159 'God's Plots', *Listener*, 7 December, pp. 759–60 (Muriel Spark).

160 'Old Modern', *New York Review of Books*, 26 October, pp. 27–30.

161 'Reading Shakespeare's Mind', *New York Review of Books*, 12 October, pp. 14–17.

162 'Strange Contempories', *Encounter*, vol. 28, no. 5 (May), pp. 65–70 (Wallace Stevens and Hart Crane).

163 'Tell me Lies about Vietnam . . .', *Encounter*, vol. 28, no. 1 (January) pp. 62–4 (Peter Brook's *US*).

164 'The Unconscious Eye', *Listener*, 23 November, pp. 671–3 (Ehrenzweig). Reprinted in *Modern Essays* (1971).

165 'World without End or Beginning', *Malahat Review*, vol. 1, pp. 113–29.

1968

166 *Continuities* (London: Routledge) viii, 238pp. (New York: Random House) x, 238pp. Reprints items 80, 81, 86, 87, 88, 89, 93, 96, 97, 99, 101, 106, 107, 108, 110, 117, 125,

126, 128, 129, 133, 134, 136, 139, 141, 142, 146, 147, 152, 173.

167 (Ed. with introduction and annotations), *The Poems of John Donne* (Cambridge: printed for the members of The Limited Editions Club at the University Printing House) xxvi, 199pp. (New York: Heritage, 1970). Limited to 1500 copies. Designed by John Dreyfus with wood engravings by Imre Reiner.

168 'Antimartyr', *Listener*, 13 June, pp. 778–9 (Muriel Spark). Reprinted in *Modern Essays* (1971).

169 'Antiuniversity', *Listener*, 29 February, pp. 257–9.

170 'Doing Time', *Listener*, 21 March, pp. 379–80 (J. T. Frazer).

171 'Easy, easy', *New York Review of Books*, 23 May, pp. 6–8 ('Liverpool Poets').

172 'Free Fall', *New York Review of Books*, 14 March, pp. 22–6 (W. J. Ong).

173 'Lawrence and the Apocalytpic Types', *Critical Quarterly*, vol. 10, pp. 14–38. Reprinted in *Continuities* (1968) and in Clarke, C. (ed.), *D. H. Lawrence: 'The Rainbow' and 'Women in Love': A Casebook* (London: Macmillan, 1969).

174 'Milton's Crises', *Listener*, 19 December, pp. 829–31.

175 'Novel, History and Type', *Novel*, vol. 1, pp. 231–8. Reprinted in Spilks, Mark (ed.), *Towards a Poetics of Fiction* (Bloomington, Ind.: Indiana University Press, 1977) pp. 23–30.

176 ' "Obscenity" and the "Public Interest" ', *New American Review*, vol. 3, pp. 229–44. Reprinted in *Modern Essays* (1971).

177 'Poetry and Borborygms', *Listener*, 6 June, pp. 735–6 (Burgess).

178 'Shuttlecock', *Listener*, 7 November, p. 619 (Updike).

179 'Tradition of Scrutiny', *Commentary*, vol. 46 (July) pp. 83–7.

180 (Trans, with Camillo Pennati), 'Xenia' by Eugenio Montale, *New York Review of Books*, 19 December, p. 9.

181 (Ed.), *The Metaphysical Poets: Key Essays on Metaphysical Poetry and the Major Metaphysical Poets* (Greenwich, Conn.: Fawcett) 351pp.

182 (Ed.), *Shakespeare: 'King Lear'. A Casebook* (London: Macmillan) 304pp.

183 'An American Patron', *Listener*, 6 February, pp. 178–9 (John Quinn).
184 'The IBM Shakespeare', *New York Review of Books*, 30 January, pp. 30–2 (Marvin Spevack's *Concordance*).
185 'The Incomparable Benjamin', *New York Review of Books*, 18 December, pp. 30–3. Reprinted in *Modern Essays* (1971).
186 'Marshall McLuhan Interviewed', *The Month*, n.s., vol. 41, no. 4, pp. 219–30. Reprinted in *The Oxford Reader* (1971).
187 (With Randolph Quirk), 'The Muse in Change: Notes on the New English Syllabus at University College London', *The Times Literary Supplement*, 5 June, p. 613.
188 'Necessary Persons', *Listener*, 16 January, pp. 84–5 (Iris Murdoch). Reprinted in *Modern Essays* (1971).
189 'Obscenities', *Listener*, 24 July, pp. 98–9. Reprinted in *Modern Essays* (1971).
190 'The Structures of Fiction', *Modern Language Notes*, vol. 84, pp. 891–915. Reprinted in Macksey, R. (ed.), *Velocities of Change: Critical Essays from MLN* (Baltimore: Johns Hopkins University Press, 1974) pp. 179–203.
191 'The University and Social Justice', *Listener*, 12 June, p. 833.
192 'When Human Nature Changed', *Listener*, 27 February, pp. 280–1 (the Edwardian period).

1970

193 'Critical List', *New York Review of Books*, 13 August, pp. 31–3 (Mary McCarthy, Philip Rahv).
194 'Foreword to the 1970 Impression', *The Romantic Agony* by Mario Praz, trans. Angus Davidson (London: Oxford University Press) pp. v–ix.
195 'Forster', *Listener*, 18 June, pp. 833–4. Reprinted in Miller, Karl (ed.), *A Listener Anthology* (1970).
196 'Is an Elite Necessary?', *Listener*, 29 October, pp. 572–6; 5 November, pp. 619–23; 12 November, pp. 651–4.
197 'A New Era in Shakespeare Criticism?', *New York Review of Books*, 5 November, pp. 33–8.
198 'The Poet in Praise of Limestone', *Atlantic Monthly*, vol.

225 (May) pp. 67–71 (Auden). Reprinted in *Modern Essays* (1971).

199 Preface, *The Golden Chain* by Anthony Rossiter (London: Gollancz), pp. ix–xi.

200 'Sheerer Spark', *Listener*, 24 September, pp. 425–7.

201 'La vie et l'oeuvre de William Butler Yeats', *Théâtre* by W.B. Yeats, trans. Madeleine Gilbert (Paris) pp. 23–56.

202 'The Young and the Elders', *Partisan Review*, vol. 37, pp. 184–98. Reprinted in Hassan, Ihab (ed.), *Liberations: New Essays on the Humanities in Revolution* (Middletown, Conn.: Wesleyan University Press, 1971).

1971

203 *Modern Essays* (London: Collins/Fontana) 352pp. Reprints several essays already collected in *Puzzles and Epiphanies* (1962) and *Continuities* (1968) together with items 164, 168, 176, 178, 185, 188, 189, 198.

204 (Ed. with Richard Poirier), *The Oxford Reader: Varieties of Contemporary Discourse* (New York: Oxford University Press) xiv, 888pp. Shorter edn, xii, 612pp. Reprints item 186.

205 *Shakespeare, Spenser, Donne. Renaissance Essays* (London: Routledge) vi, 306pp. (New York: Viking) viii, 308pp. Also as *Renaissance Essays: Shakespeare, Spenser, Donne* (London: Collins/Fontana, 1973). Reprints items 25, 53, 55, 65, 71, 90, 103, 104, 109, 123.

206 'The Algonquin Oedipus', *Listener*, 17 January, pp. 790–1 (Burgess).

207 'Attack on the Young', *Listener*, 3 June, p. 724.

208 'Britain's Decade That Was', *Atlantic Monthly*, vol. 227 (March) pp. 96–104.

209 'The Conference Game', *Listener*, 25 February, pp. 238–40.

210 'The English Novel, circa 1907', in Brower, R. A. (ed.), *Twentieth-Century Literature in Retrospect*, Harvard English Studies 2 (Cambridge, Mass.: Harvard University Press), pp. 45–64. Reprinted in *The Art of Telling* (1983).

211 'Foreseeing the Unforeseen', *Listener*, 11 November, pp. 657–8 (Muriel Spark). Reprinted in Miller, Karl (ed.), *A Second Listener Anthology* (1973), pp. 343–4.

212 'Joseph Conrad', 'Andrew Marvell', 'Wolfgang Amadeus Mozart', entries in Kronenberger, Louis and Beck, E. M. (eds), *Atlantic Brief Lives: A Biographical Companion to the Arts* (Boston: Atlantic Monthly Press, 1971).

213 'Literature and Linguistics', *Listener*, 2 December, pp. 769–71. See correspondence in *Listener*, 16 December, pp. 843–4; 23 December, pp. 874–5; 30 December, pp. 905–6; 6 January 1972, p. 19.

214 'On "Lawrence up-tight" (by Mark Spilka)', *Novel*, vol. 5, pp. 55–8 (part of a critical exchange). See *Novel*, vol. 4, pp. 252–67.

215 'A Queer Business', *Atlantic Monthly*, vol. 228 (November), pp. 140–4 (Forster).

216 'The Zero Answer', *Listener*, 8 July, pp. 53–4 (Monique Wittig).

1972

217 *Novel and Narrative* (Glasgow: University of Glasgow Press) 31pp., W. P. Ker Lecture, no. 24. Reprinted in Halperin, J. L. (ed.), *Theory of the Novel* (New York, 1974); and in *The Art of Telling* (1983).

218 *Il sense della fine: Studi sulla teoria del romanzo*, trans. Giorgio Montefoschi (Milan: Rizzoli) 216pp. (see item 157).

219 'Bob Dylan: The Metaphor at the End of the Tunnel', *Esquire*, vol. 77 (May) pp. 109–18.

220 'The British Novel Lives', *Atlantic Monthly*, vol. 230 (July) pp. 85–8 (Muriel Spark, Iris Murdoch, William Golding, Kingsley Amis).

221 'Faithing and Blithing', *Listener*, 26 October, pp. 551–2 (Auden).

222 'The Good Lord Goodman', *Listener*, 4 May, pp. 591–2.

223 'Rhythmical Grumbling', *Atlantic Monthly*, vol. 229 (January) pp. 89, 92 (T. S. Eliot).

224 'Shakespeare in the Movies', *New York Review of Books*, 4 May, pp. 18–21.

1973

225 *Lawrence* (London: Collins/Fontana) 156pp. (New York: Viking) xviii, 174pp. Modern Masters Series, General Editor, Frank Kermode.

226 *The Oxford Anthology of English Literature*, General Editors: Frank Kermode and John Hollander. Vol. 1: *The Middle Ages through the Eighteenth Century (Medieval English Literature*, ed. J. B. Trapp; *The Literature of Renaissance England*, eds. John Hollander and Frank Kermode; *The Restoration and the Eighteenth Century*, ed. M. Price). Vol. 2: *1800 to the Present (Romantic Poetry and Prose* and *Victorian Poetry and Prose*, eds. H. Bloom and L. Trilling; *Modern British Literature*, eds. Frank Kermode and John Hollander) (New York: Oxford University Press) xxx, 2376pp.; xxxii, 2238pp. (also in six paperbound volumes corresponding to the six parts).

227 'Crisis Critic', *New York Review of Books*, 17 May, pp. 37–9 (M. Faucault).

228 'Facets, Bubbles, Phylacteries', *New Statesman*, 4 May, pp. 660–1 (Roland Barthes).

229 'The Novels of D. H. Lawrence', in Spender, Stephen (ed.), *D. H. Lawrence: Novelist, Poet, Prophet*, London: Weidenfeld & Nicolson pp. 77–89.

230 'Poetry à la mode', *Atlantic Monthly*, vol. 231 (January) pp. 88–91 (*The New Oxford Book of Verse*).

231 'Policy and Pageantry', *New Statesman*, 30 November, pp. 813–4 (Renaissance spectacle).

232 'The Use of the Codes', in Chatman, Seymour (ed.), *Approaches to Poetics* (New York: Columbia University Press) pp. 51–79. Reprinted in *The Art of Telling* (1983).

233 'W. H. Auden 1907–1973', *New Statesman*, 5 October, p. 479.

1974

234 (Ed. with introductions to the Shakespeare tragedies), *The Riverside Shakespeare*, eds. G. Blackmore Evans, Harry

Levin, Herschel Baker, Ann Barton, Frank Kermode, Hallett Smith and Marie Edel (Boston: Houghton Mifflin) xviii, 1923pp.

235 (with S. Fenden and K. Palmer), *English Renaissance Literature: Introductory Lectures* (London: Gray Mills) 145pp. (Spenser, Donne, Milton).

236 'The Classic', *University of Denver Quarterly*, vol. 9, pp. 1–33.

237 '*Cymbeline* at Stratford', *The Times Literary Supplement*, 5 July, p. 710.

238 'Hawthorne's Modernity', *Partisan Review*, vol. 41, no. 3, pp. 428–41.

239 'Imperialism into Augustanism', *Hebrew University Studies in Literature and the Arts*, vol. 2, no. 2, pp. 117–50.

240 'A Modern Way with the Classic', *New Literary History*, vol. 5, no. 3, pp. 415–34.

241 'Novels: Recognition and Deception', *Critical Inquiry*, vol. 1, pp. 103–21. Reprinted in *The Art of Telling* (1983).

242 'Peter Ure, 1919–1969', in *Yeats and Anglo-Irish Literature* by Peter Ure, ed. C. J. Rawson (Liverpool: Liverpool University Press), pp. 1–39.

1975

243 *The Classic* (London: Faber and Faber); and as *The Classic: Literary Images of Permanence and Change* (New York: Viking) 141pp.

244 *How We Read Novels* (Southampton: Southampton University Press) 22pp., The Fourth Gwilyim James Memorial Lecture. Reprinted in *The Art of Telling* (1983).

245 (Ed. with an introduction), *Selected Prose of T. S. Eliot* (London: Faber and Faber; New York: Harcourt (Farrar, Straus and Giroux)) 320pp.

246 Foreword, *Semiology* by Pierre Guiraud, trans. George Cross (London: Routledge).

247 'Milton in Old Age', *Southern Review*, vol. 11, no. 3, pp. 513–29.

248 'The Model of a Modern Modernist', *New York Review of Books*, 1 May, pp. 20–3 (Peter Hanke).

249 'A Reply to Denis Donoghue', *Critical Inquiry*, vol. 1, pp. 699–700. See *Critical Inquiry*, vol. 1 (1974), pp. 447–52.

1976

250 'Diana of the Crossroads', *New Statesman*, 17 December, pp. 746–7 (Muriel Spark).
251 'Fighting Freud', *New York Review of Books*, 29 April, pp. 39–41 (F. Crews).
252 'Poet and Dancer before Diaghilev', *Salmagundi*, vol. 33–4, pp. 23–47.
253 'A Successful Alchemist', *New York Review of Books*, 14 October, pp. 6–10 (Yourcenar).
254 'Can We Say Absolutely Anything We Like?', in Anderson, Quentin, Donadio, Stephen and Marcus, Steven (eds), *Art, Politics and Will: Essays in Honor of Lionel Trilling* (New York: Basic Books) pp. 159–72. Reprinted in *The Art of Telling* (1983).

1978

255 'Another Auden', *Yale Review*, vol. 67, no. 4, pp. 609–14.
256 'A Reply to Joseph Frank', *Critical Inquiry*, vol. 4, pp. 579–88. See *Critical Inquiry*, vol. 4 (1977) pp. 231–52.
257 'Sensing Endings', *Nineteenth-Century Fiction*, vol. 33, pp. 144–58.
258 'Yes, Santa, there is a Virginia', *New York Review of Books*, 21 December, pp. 31–2 (Woolf).

1979

259 *The Genesis of Secrecy: On the Interpretation of Narrative* (Cambridge, Mass.: Harvard University Press) xvi, 169pp., The Charles Eliot Norton Lectures, 1977–8.
260 Foreword, *The Tragic Effect: The Oedipus Complex in Tragedy* by André Green, trans. Alan Sheridan (Cambridge: Cambridge University Press) pp. ix–xiii.

261 'Institutional Control of Interpretation', *Salmagundi*, vol. 43, pp. 72–86.
262 'Judgement in Venice', *Listener*, 26 April, pp. 584–5 (Spark).
263 'No wasps in India', *Listener*, 25 January, pp. 171–2 (Forster).

1980

264 'Dwelling Poetically in Connecticut', in Doggett, Frank and Buttell, Robert (eds), *Wallace Stevens: A Celebration* (Princeton, NJ: Princeton University Press) pp. 256–73.
265 'Figures in the Carpet: On Recent Theories of Narrative Discourse', *Comparative Criticism*, vol. 2, pp. 291–301.
266 'Secrets and Narrative Sequence', *Critical Inquiry*, vol. 7, no. 1, pp. 83–101. Reprinted in Mitchell, W. J. T. (ed.), *On Narrative* (Chicago: University of Chicago Press); and in *The Art of Telling* (1983).
267 'The Tempest', *The Times Literary Supplement*, 16 May, p. 553.

1981

268 Review of *The Art of Biblical Narrative* by Robert Alter, *New York Times Book Review*, July 19, p. 6.
269 Review of *Interpretation: An Essay in the Philosophy of Literary Criticism* by P. D. Juhl, *London Review of Books*, vol. 7, 20 May. Reprinted in *The Art of Telling* (1983).

1982

270 'Interpretive Continuities and the New Testament', *Raritan*, vol. 1, no. 4, pp. 33–49.
271 'On Being an Enemy to Humanity', *Raritan*, vol. 2, no. 2, pp. 87–102.
272 'Reply to Jonathan Arac', *Salmagundi*, vol. 55, pp. 156–62.
273 Review of *The Great Code: The Bible and Literature* by

Northrop Frye, *New Republic*, vol. 186, no. 23, pp. 30–3.
274 'Sacred Space', *New York Review of Books*, 21 October, pp. 39–41 (Christian verse).

1983

275 *The Art of Telling: Essays on Fiction* (Cambridge, Mass.: Harvard University Press); and as *Essays on Fiction* (London: Routledge) 229pp. Reprints items 201, 217, 232, 241, 244, 254, 266, 269.
276 'The Common Reader', *Daedalus*, vol. 112, no. 1, pp. 1–11.
277 'Opinion in *Troilus and Cressida*' in Kappeler, Susanne and Bryson, Norman (eds), *Teaching the Text* (London: Routledge) pp. 164–79.
278 'Two Instances of Interpretation (Biblical Narrative and Modern Poetics)', *Hebrew University Studies in Literature*, vol. 11, no. 1, pp. 1–19.
279 Review of *Decadent Societies* by R. M. Adams, *New York Times Book Review*, 3 July, pp. 7+.
280 Review of *Freud and Man's Soul* by Bruno Bettelheim, New York Times Book Review, 6 February, pp. 9+.
281 Review of *The Odes of John Keats* by Helen Vendler, *New York Times Book Review*, 27 November, pp. 9+.
282 'Shakespeare for the Eighties', *New York Review of Books*, 28 April, pp. 30–33.

1984

283 'The Augustan Idea', *Kenyon Review*, vol. 6, no. 2, pp. 132–5.
284 'Panel Discussion 2', in Warner, Eric (ed.), *Virginia Woolf: A Centenary Perspective* (New York: St Martin's).
285 'Les Poètes Maudits', *Partisan Review*, vol. 51, no. 1, pp. 138–43 (Blackmur, Berryman, Eileen Simpson, Lowell).

1985

286 *Forms of Attention* (The Wellek Library Lectures at the University of California at Irvine) (Chicago: University of Chicago Press) 93pp.
287 'Apocalypse and the Modern', in Friedlander, Saul, et al. (eds), *Visions of Apocalypse: End or Rebirth?* (New York: Holmes) pp. 84–106 (Lawrence).
288 'The Decline of the Man of Letters', *Partisan Review*, vol. 52, no. 3, pp. 195–209.
289 'Freud and Interpretation', *International Review of Psychoanalysis*, vol. 12, no. 1, pp. 3–12.
290 'King Lear' in Quinn, Edward (ed.), *The Shakespeare Hour: A Companion to the PBS-TV Series* (New York: New American Library), pp. 127–153.
291 Review of books on the apocalypse, *Renaissance Quarterly*, vol. 38, no. 3, pp. 554–7.
292 Review of *Flaubert's Parrot* by Julian Barnes, *New York Review of Books*, 25 April, pp. 15–16.
293 Review of *Habitations of the World* by W. H. Gass, *New York Times Book Review*, 10 March, p. 12.
294 Review of *Poetry and Politics in the English Renaissance* by David Norbrooke, *The Times Literary Supplement*, 18 January, pp. 65–6.

1986

295 (Ed.), *The Figure in the Carpet, and Other Stories* by Henry James (London: Penguin Classics) 453pp.
296 'The Plain Sense of Things' in Hartman, Geoffrey and Budick, Sanford (eds), *Midrash and Literature* (New Haven, Conn.: Yale University Press) pp. 179–94.
297 Review of *The Calabrian Abbot: Joachim of Fiore in the History of Western Thought* by B. Mcginn, *Journal of Religion*, vol. 66, no. 3, pp. 334–6.
298 'Hemingway Hunt', *London Review of Books*, vol. 8, no. 7 (14 April) pp. 14–15.

299 'Modernisms', *London Review of Books*, vol 8, no. 9 (22 May) pp. 3–6.
300 Review of *Prodigal Sons: The New York Intellectuals and their World* by A. Bloom, *New York Times Book Review*, 27 April, pp. 12–13.

1987

301 *The Literary Guide to the Bible*, with introductions and chapters by Robert Alter and Frank Kermode (Cambridge, Mass.: Harvard University Press) 678pp.
302 Review of *The Enigma of Arrival* by V. S. Naipaul, *New York Times Book Review*, 22 March, pp. 11–12.
303 Review of *Joachim of Fiore and the Myth of the Eternal Evangel* by M. Reeves and Warick Gould, *The Times Literary Supplement*, 25 September, pp. 1054–55.

1988

304 *History and Value* (the Clarendon Lectures and the North-cliffe Lectures, 1987) (Oxford: Clarendon Press) ix, 150pp.
305 'Feast of St Thomas', *London Review of Books*, vol. 10, no. 17 (29 September) pp. 3–6 (Eliot).
306 'Literary Value and Transgression', *Raritan*, vol. 7, no. 3, pp. 34–53.
307 Review of *The Place of the Stage: License, Play and Power in Renaissance England* by S. Mullaney, *New Republic*, vol. 198, no. 9, pp. 31–4.
308 Review of *Pushkin House* by A. Bitov, *New York Times Book Review*, 3 January, p. 10.

Index